The History of

Yamaha Guitars

Over Sixty Years of Innovation

ISBN-13: 978-0-634-05326-9
ISBN-10: 0-634-05326-4

Published by:
Hal Leonard Corporation
7777 W. Bluemound Road
P.O. Box 13819
Milwaukee, WI 53213

In Australia Contact:
Hal Leonard Australia Pty. Ltd.
4 Lentara Court
Cheltenham, Victoria, 3192 Australia
Email: ausadmin@halleonard.com

Library of Congress Cataloging-in-Publication Data has been applied for.

Printed in Colombia

First Edition

Visit Hal Leonard Online at **www.halleonard.com**

CONTENTS

Design

www.doddesign.com

Photo Credits

Images provided by Yamaha Corporation except for the following:

Book Front Cover:

middle photo—Kohichiro Hiki; right photo—Jim Marshall; bottom photo—Ebet Roberts

Classical Guitars:

11 and **27** (Liona Boyd), courtesy Tim Yamaya; **24-25** (Shin-ichi Fukuda), © Victor Music Industry Co., Ltd./ Jacket provided by Mr. Kato.

Acoustic Guitars:

29 and **43** (Jimmy Page), Ross Haflin; **32** (Country Joe McDonald), Jim Marshall; **35** top photo (Elliott Smith), Ted Soqui/CORBIS; lower photo (Bob Seger), Stanley Livingston; **36** (James Taylor), Henry Diltz/CORBIS; **37** (Paul Simon), Ken Settle; **39** top photo (John Denver), Todd Kaplan/StarFile; album cover courtesy of Record Research; **40** (Lennon Dragon guitar), David Behl ©Yoko Ono; **41** (Lennon sketch), © Yoko Ono; **42** bottom photo (Bruce Springsteen), Ebet Roberts; **45** top photo (Susanna Hoffs), Ken Settle; **46** top photo (Wynonna Judd), Ebet Roberts; **46** lower photo (Suzanne Vega), Ebet Roberts; **55** (Liz Phair), Bob Hall/Wire Image

Electric Guitars:

59 and **64** (Carlos Santana), Kohichiro Hiki; **63** Guitar Player cover courtesy of Music Player Network; **65** (Carlos and John), Ebet Roberts; **66** lower photo (Paul Reynolds of Flock of Seagulls), Ken Settle; **67** lower photo (Duran Duran), Ebet Roberts; **69** upper photo (Jackson 5), Neal Preston/CORBIS; lower photo (Tito and Michael Jackson) CORBIS; **80-81** (Mike Stern), Ebet Roberts

Bass Guitars:

97 and **111** (Nathan East), StarFile; **104** (Nathan East), StarFile; **103** (Anthony and Roth), Ebet Roberts; p. 105 magazine cover courtesy of Guitar Player magazine/Music Player Network; **107** (Sheehan), Ken Settle

Creating *Kando* Together

Kando *is a Japanese word that signifies an inspired state of mind, heart, and spirit.*

Yamaha, established in 1887, has a rich history and spirit that has traversed through three centuries. One special spirit is the trait of Japanese people that allows us to take elements from different cultures, and unite and blend them together into something special. However, I feel that this precious ability is in the process of disappearing. For me, our brand slogan, "Creating Kando *Together," embraces and reconnects with many of these feelings.*

When developing instruments, it is impossible to create anything of worth if we cannot feel the Kando in what we are doing.

For example, I don't think it is going too far in saying that the origin of Yamaha Guitars can be found in the spirit of the Spanish craftsman. As told in this book, our craftsmen went off to Spain, where they spent years studying the techniques essential in the making of the guitar, and more importantly, coming to know and identify with the spirit of the Spanish craftsman. Taking these newly acquired techniques and what we learned from the craftsman's spirit, we blended and united them with the expertise in woods and cutting edge technologies that we have accumulated since our founding, into a method that allowed us to create better guitars. Through repeated trial and error and critical evaluation by professional musicians, we succeeded in crafting guitars that deeply inspired and impressed all of those who were involved in this endeavor. That is Kando.

We have long put great priority in development through collaboration with professional musicians. Communication with artists is highly valued at Yamaha, and for this purpose we have two artist relations facilities and staff: ART (previously known as R&D) in Tokyo and YGD (Yamaha Guitar Development) in Los Angeles. When the performer discovers a fine guitar they can feel Kando. When the artist playing this fine instrument moves the audience, they also feel Kando. The feeling of Kando is spread in this manner.

Spreading Kando—its meaning and feeling—throughout the world is our dream.

Shuji Ito, *president, Yamaha Corporation*

ACKNOWLEDGMENTS

This book has been the work of many individuals and groups. It has been my honor to be the author and researcher heading up this project. However, there have been immeasurable contributions from many other people in the music industry.

Although I will not be able to mention them all, I would like to acknowledge a few key people, without whom this book would never have come to be.

The staff in Hamamatsu, Japan, at the Yamaha headquarters' Guitar Division contributed endless hours of conversation, while leading me into the files and closets of Yamaha's analog records of the early days. Their staff was tireless in meeting after meeting where we researched, clarified, and confirmed the details of this previously undocumented body of work. It was there that the chronological structure of the book was born.

Yamaha Corporation of America's guitar department guided me through a mountain of historical data, photographs, and guitar designs, especially Yamaha Guitar Development's staff in Hollywood. Without their assistance, this book could not be.

Contributing author Matt Blackett interviewed numerous artists and documented their conversations in a creative and colorful way that is both interesting and factual.

I offer special thanks to all of the guitar players and designers who offered their time to converse with me about Yamaha and this book project. Particular thanks to Carlos Santana for closing the door to all interruptions while he and I discussed his powerful and musical relationship with his Yamaha "brothers" in Japan. It is the artists' contributions that make this book complete.

Hal Leonard Corporation's staff has been extraordinary in the process of pulling together the history of the largest guitar brand in the world. It is Hal Leonard Corporation's diligent attention to every detail that has made it possible for me to attempt compiling and writing a massive task such as this. It has been a privilege to be their partner and author on this project.

Lastly, thank you to my many mentors in the acoustic guitar industry who have answered question after question from me about technical and historical issues around this book.

Mark Kasulen

For the first time in more than six decades since the first Yamaha guitar was handmade, the history of Yamaha guitars has been documented.

As author, I looked deep into the activities that started Yamaha's guitar making. It was there that I found a wealth of collaborative projects that have only been recorded through the age-old oral tradition, almost like story-telling. Basically, the early days of Yamaha guitar making were captured by the memories of the builders and the players like snapshots of history.

I searched through hundreds of old documents including blueprints, patents, photographs, catalogs, and other archived hard copies of Yamaha's guitar history. From there, it was possible to glue the pieces together, one by one.

This book starts with an overview of the company history, a look at Yamaha's educational approach to bringing music to the world, and then an in-depth look at the guitars.

The structure of this book is a chronological summary of Yamaha's classical, acoustic, electric, archtop, and bass stringed instruments. You'll be able to look into each of those chapters to read about the development of Yamaha's guitars. Each chapter includes details about the building and design process, unique patents and technical developments that made Yamaha successful, full photographic representation of the instruments, and artist stories with pictures that will captivate any guitar enthusiast.

Yamaha's global approach to music and business required that a history book of this magnitude include the comments of people in all corners of the music industry. Throughout the book, you will find quotes contributed by players, builders, educators, and business people. It was through speaking with these people that I managed to pull together an international book that will speak to readers at all levels of guitar interest.

Whether you are a player looking for artist information, a luthier curious about the first electric guitar patents, a business person exploring Yamaha's manufacturing activities, or someone simply interested in the magnificent world of Yamaha guitars, this book is for you.

As a reference tool, The History of Yamaha Guitars includes many technical details along with a comprehensive Serial Number Chart. There, you will be able to determine when a particular Yamaha guitar was made.

As you journey through the pages, I sincerely hope you find the same fascination and surprise that I found in writing it.

Yamaha's Philosophy for Success

When Mr. Torakusu Yamaha formed the Nippon Gakki Co., Ltd. in 1897, little did the world know that this pioneering organ-maker's modest start-up venture would someday become the multinational conglomerate that today bears its founder's name. And ever since its humble inception over 100 years ago, the Yamaha Corporation has maintained a clear and direct approach to inspiring the world…not only through its product, but also through its mission. Having established itself as a leader in the music industry from the start—and in the guitar business in particular for the last 50-plus years—Yamaha has made its people, the culture of music, and global harmony the impetus of its operations.

Yamaha began making guitars in 1941 at its facility in Hamamatsu, Japan (where the company has been headquartered since its beginning), but experienced a break in activities during the global conflicts of WWII. In 1946, under the direction of Genichi Kawakami and his research and development team, Yamaha's guitar making began in earnest. Launched initially as a subgroup of the company's piano R&D department, the nascent guitar-manufacturing division, after being allocated its own space independent of the piano facility, became known as the Yamaha Guitar Custom Shop—which is still in operation today. The Custom Shop's small team of craftsmen, all of whom had great woodworking skills but little or no experience in guitar-building, made only minor modifications initially, such as strengthening the bracings and switching to steel strings. However, these perhaps seemingly negligible efforts gave these early luthiers-in-the-making a starting point from which today's Yamahas would eventually evolve.

The collaborative atmosphere of the early Yamaha Guitar Custom Shop is likewise intrinsic to the Yamaha company as a whole. Japanese ideology holds that the group, rather than the individual, has the greatest chance of success. Therefore, it is this community-minded, team-oriented tradition that Yamaha has steadfastly applied to all of its endeavors, including its guitar-making efforts. For more than five decades, Yamaha has reached into the luthier houses of Spain, the repair shops of the United States, and into the countless instrument stores and music halls worldwide; there, company representatives meet with top-notch guitarists to discuss new designs and construction possibilities.

Like its corporate objective, the imagery employed in Yamaha's logo reflects the company's philosophy and spirit. Featuring three tuning forks enclosed in a circle, the logo represents the cooperative relationship of Yamaha's three "pillars" of business: technology, production, and sales. (The trademark also symbolizes the three essential musical elements: melody, harmony, and rhythm.) The enclosed circle evokes not only Yamaha's robust vitality as a global example of excellence in its field, but as an entity of unity, wholeness, and integrity.

To sustain its growth throughout the 21st century, Yamaha is concertedly striving to become a truly global enterprise that helps enrich the quality of people's lives worldwide. Yamaha aims to fulfill its responsibilities as a corporation to four key groups of stakeholders—customers, shareholders, those who work with Yamaha, and society.

To Customers
Yamaha will fully satisfy the customer by offering high quality products and services. It will use new and traditional technologies—as well as creativity and artistry—and continue to be a known, trusted, and loved brand.

To Shareholders
Yamaha will increase the satisfaction and understanding of its shareholders by striving for healthy profits and returns, and by achieving productivity, using high quality, transparent management, and by practicing disclosure.

To Those Who Work with Yamaha
Yamaha will develop relationships of mutual trust with all of those who work with Yamaha in accordance with fair rules based on social norms, and strive to be an organization in which individuals can demonstrate their abilities fully, have confidence, and have pride.

To Society
Yamaha will give first priority to safety, and will care for the environment. Yamaha will be a good corporate citizen, will observe laws, and will work ethically, developing the economy and contributing to local and global culture.

This involves reinforcing corporate governance, raising the quality of services to the customer, ensuring appropriate and timely disclosure, and maintaining a harmonious balance with society and the environment.

At the advent of the new millennium, Yamaha introduced a new global marketing concept, "CREATING 'KANDO' TOGETHER." "Kando" is a Japanese term signifying an inspired state of mind, heart, and spirit, an emotion that arises when something is deeply felt. Kando, when profoundly experienced, becomes hopes and dreams. This works in well with Yamaha's business objective, as the sharing of hopes and dreams is what links people together:

Yamaha will continue to create Kando, and enrich culture with technology and passion born of sound and music, together with people all over the world.

This company's brand slogan, "CREATING 'KANDO' TOGETHER," has permeated the entire organization. Eventually, the Yamaha group hopes to integrate Kando into all of its undertakings, thereby linking people the world over in the pursuit of a richer, culturally enhanced life.

Genichi Kawakami started the first music school with the "Music Class for Pre-school Children" in Tokyo in 1945. Later this class developed into the Yamaha Music School, designed to teach music from the fundamental.

Mr. Kawakami (1912-2002) was the president of Nippon Gakki Co., Ltd. (predecessor of the Yamaha Corporation) from 1950-1977 and 1989-1993. A graduate of Takachiho College of Commerce, he started working for Yamaha in 1937 where his father had been president since 1927.

In 1950 he took over his father's position as president of the musical instrument company that had been established in 1887, and developed it into the world's largest maker of pianos, fueling a music boom in Japan.

According to Mr. Kawakami, after a 90-day "observing" tour around the world in 1953, he was deeply inspired to bring music education to Japanese families. Mr. Kawakami had observed people's leisure activities and became convinced that the recreational market would rebound in post-war Japan.

Yamaha has established music schools in Japan and more than 40 countries around the world. Yamaha's system of music education now encompasses more than 530,000 students with 15,000 teachers at 6,000 locations in Japan. An additional 170,000 students are enrolled in 1,600 schools around the world.

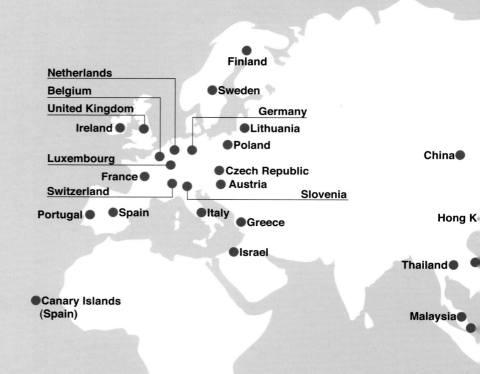

Thus, Mr. Kawakami wanted music education to be widely available and affordable. As Mr. Kawakami explained, he wanted to integrate music into family life because of its importance in the role of human development.

In the 1950s, music was taught through private lessons from teachers who were graduates of music colleges – a system employed both in Japan and abroad. Mr. Kawakami created a music education system focused around group instruction to fulfill his wish that as many people as possible be exposed to the joy of a music-filled life.

The public rapidly adopted Mr. Kawakami's innovative ideas as his pilot classes began in 1954. By 1966 his music education program had expanded to 5,200 schools with 2,800 teachers and 230,000 students. The first international music school opened in the United States in 1965. Mr. Kawakami's vision of a "life filled with music should be extended to all children of the world" was realized.

Structure of Yamaha's Music Education

Underlying Yamaha's unique music education system are three principles: timely education, group lessons, and an emphasis on creativity.

Timely Education
In order for children to enjoy music, it is effective to give them appropriate guidance within the realm of their capacity and development. Based upon the concept of timely education, Yamaha Music Education introduces pre-school age children to music fundamentals at a time when their ability to discern pitch and identify sounds is ripening. Children at this level of development are poised to learn the basic music elements of rhythm, melody, and harmony through the singing and playing of instruments.

Group Lessons
Group lessons enable children to enjoy rich musical experiences as well as extra-musical experiences such as making friends and learning about group dynamics in the context of ensembles.

Emphasis on Creativity
To enable students to nourish their creativity, Yamaha's music education system helps them develop sensitivity and imagination – sources of creativity.

What comes to mind when I think of Yamaha guitars is…perfection.

Yamaha was the first company to approach me about designing a particular guitar suited for my needs. I was honored and delighted with the results.

There were actually two guitars, one in 1982 and one in 1985. A representative from Yamaha's Custom Shop in Japan came to see me in Toronto, Canada. We agreed that I was looking for a very resonant guitar and a particular sound. He took thorough measurements and promised to find the perfect woods. Nothing was too much trouble.

I remember the thrill and excitement when the guitars finally arrived. Both of them were extremely delicate. The sound was perfect for me. The workmanship was truly amazing.

I've always recommended Yamaha guitars to my students. Yamaha has made instruments that are playable, beautiful, and affordable for students around the world.

Guitar, for me, has always been great therapy. I think that there is a spiritual quality to classical music in general. The guitar is relaxing. Its sounds are so beautiful. Yamaha has contributed to the proliferation and interest in both guitars and music around the world.

I once had the opportunity to play a small concert for the King and Queen of Spain and their guests. I remember thinking, "Oh my, here I am playing for the King and Queen of the country that is most famous for making the classical guitar." My Yamaha sounded beautiful! When I was finished, there were many compliments.

There is still no sound more beautiful than that which comes from just those six strings. That's the classical guitar. And it is hard to beat.

Yamaha has played a significant role in music around the world, especially in their contributions to classical music and guitar. It is more important now than ever.

I thank them for their generosity.

– Liona Boyd

Classical Guitars

The History of Yamaha Guitars

Dynamic
Guitar S50

Top	Spruce
Back/Sides	Maple
Neck	Nato
Fingerboard	Bubinga
Bridge	Bubinga

Production Begins

As stated earlier, the research and development of Yamaha guitars began at the Yamaha Hamamatsu facility in Japan with a small team of craftsmen in the early 1940s.

In the middle 1940s, Yamaha guitar production began. Yamaha's designers put steel strings on a nylon-string guitar. Dynamic guitar production continued to the beginning of the 1970s. The steel strings on the guitar put too much tension on the bridge bond and top bracing structure. In fact, the whole instrument would be stressed beyond normal structural design capabilities; so to safely handle these stresses, after the initial top-bracing structure was adjusted, one bolt was installed at the center of the bridge, directly through the top of the guitar. It was a small nut, bolt, and washer tightened down to add extra strength to the bridge-to-top bond. In the photo, there is a mother-of-pearl dot in the bridge that covers the bolt. This technique became an industry standard for covering bridge bolts when they are used. Fortunately, current instrument designs have almost eliminated the need for bridge bolts.

In the late 1940s, Yamaha began the research and development necessary to build a guitar factory. A factory was created in Hamamatsu in order to begin a production line for guitar making.

During the 1950s, Yamaha classical guitars were sold within Japan through the retail shops that Yamaha

had established for piano sales. There was no significant product success in the market other than the fact that Yamaha guitars were finally on the market.

In 1950, the famous Japanese guitarist Yasumasa Obara advised Yamaha in their classical guitar designs. In 1952, the first CG guitars were made.

Mr. Eduardo Ferrer Comes from Spain to Collaborate with the New Custom Shop

In 1966, the Custom Shop was officially established. One of the first projects was the collaborative work with Eduardo Ferrer, a traditional classical builder from Spain who came to assist the Yamaha Custom Shop with its design and creation of classical guitars. For three six-week periods over the course of two years, Mr. Ferrer worked with the Yamaha builders to explore classical building techniques and apply those techniques to Yamaha guitars. This interaction was foundational to the development of the Custom Shop, the fruit of which appeared in models GC5, GC7, and GC10.

Yamaha's first production facility for guitars in Hamamatsu, Japan.

Spanish luthier Eduardo Ferrer comes to the Yamaha Custom Shop.

GC5

Mr. Nakabayashi-tested guitar, GC5

Top	Spruce
Back/Sides	Jacaranda
Neck	Mahogany
Fingerboard	Ebony
Bridge	Jacaranda

The Evaluation System

In 1967, the models GC5, GC7, and GC10 were the first creations out of Yamaha's Custom Shop. Unfortunately, the builders at Yamaha had no experience in evaluating guitars. To solve this problem, Yamaha enlisted a professional classical guitar player in Japan to work with the craftsmen during the final inspection process. He would play an instrument, make a professional judgment about the sound quality of the guitar, and subsequently apply a model number, which was determined by the sound quality of the instrument. After the determination of sound quality, the craftsmen would apply one of three different peghead faces to each instrument, producing three different models with three different prices—instruments which differed only in sound quality and peghead face appearance.

Export Begins

After almost 20 years of learning and refining, along with the presence of a manufacturing facility that could offer a consistently quality product, Yamaha was able to begin exporting guitars. In 1966, the first exports included the GC models, and Yamaha also offered the less expensive factory models G50, G60, G80, G100, G120, and G160. These guitars were made with maple back and sides, nato necks, and bubinga or rosewood fingerboards and bridges (all of these woods are in the same family as their more expensive custom-shop counterparts, but are less expensive to purchase). Each of the models was similar in construction, differing only in rosette marquetry and binding configuration.

GC5 and GC10. The only difference was in sound quality and peghead face appearance.

Mr. Atsumasa Nakabayashi play-testing a guitar

Also in the mid 1960s, the flamenco guitar designs were introduced into the Custom Shop's R&D work. Flamenco guitars are similar in construction to classic guitars, but have a lighter bracing and are generally made with cypress back and sides. The GC5F, GC7F, and GC10F models were built in the traditional flamenco style with the same classic specs, except for the cypress material used on the back and sides, and the inclusion of different tuning machines and binding.

The first requinto guitar (essentially a smaller classical guitar) was built in the Custom Shop in four models: GC7R, GC8R, GC12R, and GC13R.

In 1969, the Yamaha Corporation merged with a local stringed instrument manufacturer called Tenryu Gakki Corp. Yamaha Corp. changed the name to Yamaha Corporation Wada Factory.

Flamenco model GC10F

Top	**Spruce**
Back/Sides	**Cypress**
Neck	**Mahogany**
Fingerboard	**Ebony**
Bridge	**Jacaranda**

G50

G120

G160

Yamaha's first export guitars: G50, G120, and G160.

Yamaha's Taiwan Manufacturing Facility Opens

At the start of the acoustic folk boom in the 1960s, Yamaha saw an opportunity to invest in a manufacturing facility in Taiwan and produce greater quantities of guitars at more economical prices. In 1970, Kaohsiung Yamaha was opened and became one of the world's largest manufacturers of guitars—and continues to make guitars today.

The first series of guitars that came off the production line were the G55A through G255A models. These were economical classical guitars that utilized traditional manufacturing techniques, classical specifications, and existing designs. By using alternative materials, such as agathis instead of mahogany for the back and sides, Yamaha was able to make these guitars more affordable.

Additionally, the three-quarter-sized model G40 was also made in Taiwan. This was Yamaha's first exploration into the student-size guitar market. The overall length and size were smaller than that of a normal guitar.

G55A

Top	**Spruce**
Back/Sides	**Agatis**
Neck	**Nato**
Fingerboard	**Bubinga**
Bridge	**Bubinga**

G40 student-size guitar.

Yamaha manufacturing facility, Kaohsiung, Taiwan.

Manuel Hernandez Collaboration

Similar to Yamaha's work with Mr. Ferrer in the 1960s, in the 1970s, Yamaha explored collaborative work with Manuel Hernandez, the famous Spanish classical guitar builder. As Hideyuki Ezaki of Yamaha's Custom Shop explains it, they knew that the Spanish building techniques and designs of Antonio De Torres influenced much of the Spanish building community. Yamaha explored this lineage from Jose Pernas to Antonio De Torres, and then to the Alias styles of building. Further on in this Spanish classical guitar development, other generations emerged. In that history, both Eduardo Ferrer and Manuel Hernandez built a reputation for themselves as designers and builders of classical guitars worldwide. Another was Mr. Barvero, who influenced what Yamaha's guitar-makers built.

In 1973, for about a month and a half, Manuel Hernandez came to Yamaha in Hamamatsu and worked with the men in the Custom Shop to develop their skills as classical guitar builders. Once their work together was completed, Yamaha decided to incorporate their knowledge of the three Spanish building techniques into the hand-craftsmanship of three Yamaha luthiers.

GC30A

GC30B

Top	**Cedar**
Back/Sides	**Jacaranda**
Neck	**Mahogany**
Fingerboard	**Ebony**
Bridge	**Jacaranda**

The GC30-10:
a ten-string
classical guitar

Top	**German Spruce**
Back/Sides	**Jacaranda**
Neck	**Mahogany**
Fingerboard	**Ebony**
Bridge	**Jacaranda**

At this time, Yamaha utilized a group-building technique and defined three styles of classical guitar-building technique. The first one was the "Yamaha style," which mixed several techniques with the Japanese style. The second was the "Hernandez style." The third was the "Barberos." The differences in building and design nuance had to do with neck-joint, bracing, and sound differences. Those three styles took on the model number suffixes A, B, and C ("A" for Yamaha style, "B" for Hernandez style, and "C" for Barberos style). At that time, the Yamaha Custom Shop had three significant builders: Mr. Magosaku Suzuki, Mr. Youichiro Suzuki, and Mr. Tokio Iguchi. These three men built each of the A, B, and C models of guitars; so, at any one time in the building process, there could have been nine combinations: each man building all three styles. These three men and their individual workmanship made it possible for nine specific and different tonal characteristics to be produced through the three models. Although originally a great idea for sales and marketing, the process of labeling the guitars separately for each model and each man who built it caused a demand in the market that was too cumbersome for Yamaha to supply. For example, some players liked the Hernandez style built by Suzuki, while others liked the Yamaha style built by Iguchi, etc. Eventually, this process needed to be eliminated and the guitars were instead built by the group in order to eliminate the confusion of nine different sounds.

The effort was an attempt to utilize the unique workmanship skills of each man, and to encourage each to develop his own techniques in lutherie. Unfortunately, from a marketing and sales perspective, it did not work.

Narciso Yepes Collaboration

Narciso Yepes is a globally famous classic guitarist who was the pioneer of ten-string guitar performance. In 1969, while in Japan, he visited the Yamaha Ginza store. There he saw the GC10, which started his interest and relationship with Yamaha. In May of 1971, he began evaluating more Yamaha guitars and advising the R&D team on 10-string guitars.

When Yepes visited the Yamaha head office in 1974, they had a product for him to evaluate. Yamaha had built him a 10-string guitar with a spruce top. Yepes liked the guitar so much he requested a 10-string cedar top model to evaluate on his next visit. On his next visit he evaluated two GC30A type 10-string guitars. He said, "These new trial products are better than the last one; I would like to buy one of them."

Yamaha offered to give Yepes the guitar if he agreed to use it in concert. He would not accept the present because he always bought the guitars he played. Yamaha had not established a price for the guitar and had to come up with the price on the spot. He purchased the guitar for 300,000 Japanese Yen.

When famous Japanese guitar players Kiyoshi Shoumura and Hoshido Mikio went to Spain to study guitar under Yepes, Yepes saw they were playing a Ramirez guitar, and Yepes asked, "Why don't you play a Yamaha guitar? I have bought a Yamaha guitar myself because I know Yamaha produces very good guitars."

Matsu & Sugi

In the Japanese language, *matsu* means spruce and *sugi* means cedar. During the mid-1970s, Yamaha's Hamamatsu factory began manufacturing a series of classical guitars with the model numbers GC5M, GC7M, GC10M, GC15M, and GC20M. Additionally, the same models with the suffix "S" (as in "GC5S") were built and sold. The "M" denoted that the guitar featured a *matsu* or spruce top, while the "S" denoted a *sugi* or cedar top.

By 1977, Yamaha's Taiwan facility was able to obtain solid top materials, and manufacture economical guitars with solid, book-matched tops. Book-matched tops had been the industry standard for quality instruments for hundreds of years, and this feature now enabled the company to offer an even higher quality product at an affordable price. The first model to have a solid top was the G245S.

Narciso Yepes

G245S

Top	Spruce
Back/Sides	Rosewood
Neck	Nato
Fingerboard	Rosewood
Bridge	Rosewood

GC10M

Top	Spruce
Back/Sides	Rosewood
Neck	Mahogany
Fingerboard	Rosewood
Bridge	Rosewood

Maestro Segovia and
Yamaha designer/luthier
Toshio Kato in
Segovia's Madrid studio.

David Bergstrom, future
Yamaha employee, with
Andrés Segovia at the
master's home in
Madrid, Spain.

Maestro Andrés Segovia Connection

Andrés Segovia, the world's first and leading Maestro of classical guitar at the time, worked with Yamaha's builders to evaluate Yamaha's classical guitars. One of Yamaha's executives, Mr. Hishinuma, showed the Maestro a GC30A custom guitar. His comments were positive.

In 1980, Mr. Kato and Mr. Ezaki, who were classical guitar designers, visited Segovia's home in Madrid. The GC70 cedar-top model, which they brought along with them, was well received by the Maestro. He subsequently added it to his ten-piece collection of guitars. Once again, in 1982, Yamaha's designers visited Segovia after a performance in Hamburg, Germany. Of the two guitars that they brought, Segovia extolled the GC71, and later played it in a concert hall. Finally, in 1982, Yamaha's staff visited Segovia's home for the last time and showed him a few guitars. Of them, the cedar-top GC70 was the guitar that Segovia selected and kept in his cottage.

Another Yamaha–Segovia Connection

Yamaha has had an interesting journey through the decades with the late Maestro Andrés Segovia. Not only did the Yamaha Custom Shop builders make a few trips to be with the Maestro and work on the design and development of classical guitars, but the future Yamaha Corporation of America's Corporate Planning Manager, Mr. David Bergstrom, studied with Andrés Segovia for three consecutive summers.

Bergstrom explained that, in 1979 while finishing his Master's Degree at SMU in Texas, he had the opportunity to see Segovia play and to meet him in person. During that interaction, Bergstrom was invited to study with Segovia at his home in Madrid.

Bergstrom recalls: "Segovia would not let students bring our guitars into his fourth-floor studio. Their place was like a museum, with paintings and art from famous artists all over the world.

"He offered me a Yamaha guitar on which to play. It was not until I joined Yamaha that I discovered that the Japanese Yamaha staff was working with him at that exact time, refining the design of a finely made, handcrafted concert guitar. I was very impressed with the quality of sound and construction, and played for Segovia on that exact Yamaha guitar!"

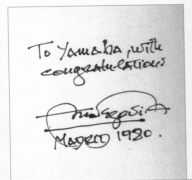

Yamaha Music Manufacturing Indonesia (YMMI) facility.

Yamaha Music Craft guitar manufacturing facility in Hamamatsu, Japan.

"Though I met with the Maestro at events over the years, I never really discussed my decision to pursue a career in the music business; but I believe he would have understood."

Yamaha's Custom Shop introduced the new custom models GC50, GC60, GC61, and GC62 to replace the GC30A, B, and C models that were covered earlier in this chapter. These models are still made today.

The Japanese Hamamatsu Wada factory finally stopped production in 1985, and closed completely in 1987. The Taiwan facility picked up all of the Wada facility production, including the manufacture of the G50, CG110, and CG190S.

New Production Facilities

YMMI, or Yamaha Music Manufacturing Indonesia, became Yamaha's newest endeavor to lower the cost of manufacturing and bring economical guitars to the world market. As Indonesia was quickly becoming the next country where manufacturing was possible for stringed instruments, the combination of labor costs and material supply within that country made it a perfect venue for manufacturing an economical product. Additionally, the indigenous woods in Indonesia could be used in the manufacturing of guitars. Production started with the C40 and the C60, which began a new generation of the most affordable, quality nylon-string guitars in the guitar industry.

Yamaha Music Craft (YMC) was established as the Hamamatsu, Japan, guitar production facility in 1997. It combined hand-craftsmanship with manufacturing to make a production version of what the Custom Shop built. Through many changes in the industry's manufacturing, and the gap between Yamaha's Custom Shop in Hamamatsu and the manufacturing in the Taiwan factory, it was the next logical step to create a manufacturing facility that incorporated the old-world hand-craftsmanship with some of the high-technology machinery to make a more intricate guitar at an affordable price. For the first few years, this new facility made only steel-string acoustics. Eventually, in the year 2000, the first market-ready nylon-string guitars were manufactured. The GC21, GC31, and GC41, along with their cedar-top counterparts, the GC21C, GC31C, and GC41C, were manufactured and sold. Also, the GCX31C was introduced with an acoustic electric cutaway.

The Silent Guitar

Through extraordinary research in the realm of contemporary guitarists' needs and performance requirements with acoustic-electric amplification, in 2001, Yamaha created the "Silent Guitar," model number SLG100N.

This instrument incorporates state-of-the-art electronics in guitar amplification, ergonomic designs that are both comfortable and appealing, and a never-seen-before design. Players around the world are turning to the Silent Guitar as an alternative to the normal, full-sized instrument for performance and practice.

Silent Guitar

SLG100N

Neck	**Mahogany**
Fingerboard	**Rosewood**
Bridge	**Rosewood**

CGS Series

Classical Guitars for Students

Yamaha has always supported global music education. Violins, keyboards, and many other instruments are made by Yamaha, particularly for children of all ages. The CGS Series (Classical Guitars for Students) includes three sizes of classical guitars to accommodate students who are not ready for full-sized instruments. The specifications are proportioned to create a comfortable and easy-playing feel for students. The intonation and setup specs allow for easy playing, even for young fingers.

Yamaha's classical guitar chapter is not yet over. For almost 60 years, Yamaha has been refining and developing the art and craft of classical guitar making. Those efforts continue, as the designers and builders of Yamaha classical guitars search for a more perfect instrument for players around the world.

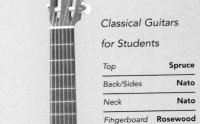

Classical Guitars for Students

Top	Spruce
Back/Sides	Nato
Neck	Nato
Fingerboard	Rosewood
Bridge	Rosewood

Yamaha Music Craft's first classical guitar, the CG31

Top	Hokkaido Spruce
Back/Sides	Rosewood
Neck	Mahogany
Fingerboard	Ebony
Bridge	Rosewood

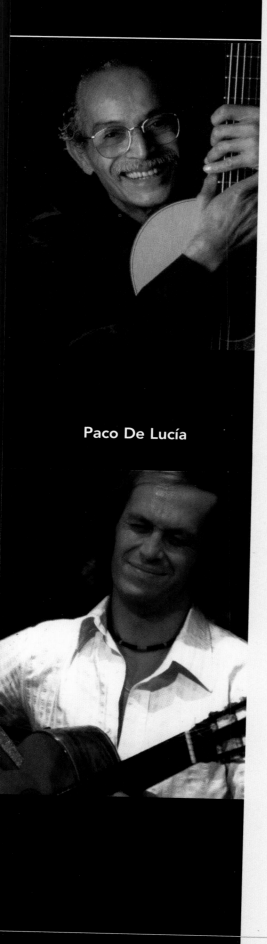

Baden Powell

Paco De Lucía

Yamaha's International Players

Baden Powell

Baden Powell was globally famous as the bossa nova guitarist and composer of Brazilian music. Mr. Naniki, designer of the GC71, visited Powell in a concert hall in Hamburg, Germany, in 1984, where Powell evaluated the guitar. Mr. Naniki later visited Powell's house with another test piece of the GC71. Powell loved the GC71 and used it in concert guitar performances after that. A letter arrived at Yamaha from Powell in 1985. He said in the letter: "This guitar made me absentminded in concert, charmed other musicians, and greatly moved us. This is not an ordinary guitar, I can declare. Life is dwelling in this guitar."

He continued to use the GC71 until his death in 2000.

Paco de Lucía

Paco de Lucía is a world-famous flamenco guitarist. Yamaha handed him a custom-made flamenco guitar, model GC10F, in the 1970s. He was pleased. He used it and another custom-made guitar, the GC30C, in 1981. Later in 1984, he used a Yamaha guitar with a pickup: model GC70.

Leo Browel

Leo Browel, a popular composer of guitar music, was contacted in Europe by Yamaha in 1979. After his product evaluation, he ordered his first GC30A. He visited Yamaha's head office many times.

Eduardo Falu

Eduardo Falu is the guitar player known as the "Maestro of Folklore." He evaluated many Yamaha guitars in the 1970s. Finally, in 1981, Falu settled on a GC70, which was his favorite.

Shin-ichi Fukuda

Shin-ichi Fukuda is one of the guitarists who represents Japan today. He won the Paris International Guitar Competition in 1981. He was interested in Yamaha's custom guitars, so Yamaha's staff handed him a GC70. He recorded his debut album in 1983, using that same guitar.

Leo Browel

Eduardo Falu

Alirio Diaz

Konrad Ragossnig

Alirio Diaz

Alirio Diaz is a well-known Venezuelan arranger. In 1976, when he visited Yamaha to evaluate guitars with the R&D staff, he enjoyed a particular GC30A. When Mr. Kato asked him if he could play it in concert, Diaz asked for 30 minutes to test it. He did, and then took it on the road with him for his tour to Japan.

Konrad Ragossnig

Konrad Ragossnig, a prominent guitar player and professor of classical guitar, began a dialogue with Yamaha in 1977. He eventually brought both the GC30A and the GC70 from Yamaha for tours both in Japan and globally.

Atahualpa Yupanqui

Siegfried Behrend

Siegfried Behrend

Siegfried Behrend is known as a pioneer and composer in the German guitar community. Yamaha contacted him in 1976, after which he and the company began a few years of interaction before he finally found his perfect Yamaha guitar, the GC70, in 1980.

Atahualpa Yupanqui

Atahualpa Yupanqui is the Maestro of the Latin American folk music from Argentina. He visited Japan in the late 1960s. After meeting with the designers, he left with his hand-selected GC10, which was later used to record his visit-to-Japan commemorative album.

Liona Boyd

"I got my first Yamaha in 1972. It was a travelling companion, and I recorded with it in India. Since then I have used Yamaha acoustics on stage as well as on my travels. It's the quality and sound of the instruments that appeal. Thanks, Yamaha!"

– Jimmy Page

Acoustic Guitars

The History of Yamaha Guitars

The Perfect Instrumen

For hundreds of years, people the world over have been drawn to the acoustic guitar.

From the lute-playing, strolling minstrels of the Renaissance to the modern-day singer/songwriter, there's just something magical about an instrument that can be transported anywhere easily and sounds so beautiful. When pressed to choose just one instrument to have on a desert island, a huge percentage of musicians would choose the acoustic guitar. It is, quite possibly, the perfect instrument.

Yamaha was well aware of the power and the glory of the acoustic guitar when the company began producing them in the Hamamatsu Custom Shop in 1966. The music world was driven by guitar in the 1960s; and while much of the new music was fueled by electric guitars, acoustics were nonetheless the main instruments on hits by the Beatles, the Everly Brothers, and Simon & Garfunkel. The acoustic guitar was a mainstay of chart-topping country artists such as Johnny Cash, and it was certainly the weapon of choice for folk icons like Bob Dylan.

The first Yamaha steel-string acoustics—models FG150 and FG180—were released in 1966. The guitars were designed with input from top Japanese professional players. These initial guitars are in many ways emblematic of

Yamaha's first production acoustic, the FG180.

what Yamaha would come to represent to the guitar-playing world—the first. All over the world, guitarists in every style clearly remember their first guitar. And, in a startling number of cases, that first guitar was a Yamaha acoustic.

James Black, guitarist for the band Finger Eleven, recalls his first guitar. "It was Christmas morning when I was seven years old," says Black. "I had gotten up four hours before my parents and unwrapped a Yamaha acoustic. I was so excited—I remember hiding behind the couch with my new guitar so my mom wouldn't know I had spoiled the surprise. It's funny—I still get that exact same feeling every time I get a new Yamaha."

Alternative rock singer/songwriter Liz Phair recalls being drawn into guitar playing by a Yamaha: "My godfather had a Yamaha acoustic, and he would play songs for all us kids. I've always remembered that logo in the soundhole. I was entranced by that logo. When I started playing guitar in the eighth grade, it was on a Yamaha."

Jane's Addiction guitarist Dave Navarro also cut his teeth on a Yamaha. "It was a birthday present when I was eleven," he states. "I had been playing a little on this garage-sale guitar, and when it looked like I was going to stick with it, my mom got me a Yamaha acoustic. That's where it all started for me."

And that's where steel-string production started for Yamaha. After making reed organs and pianos since before the turn of the century, and with classi-cal-guitar production already in its second decade, Yamaha began turning out steel-string guitars. The FG150 and FG180 models were followed in 1967 by the company's first 12-string acoustic, the FG230.

The FG230: Yamaha's first production 12-string.

Woodstock

*Gimme an FG!
Country Joe
McDonald playing
for a few friends in
upstate New York on
August 15, 1969.*

In 1969, Yamaha began exporting guitars to the U.S. and Europe.

This would allow Yamaha to step up production and increase sales. It also exposed new models such as the FG140 and FG150 to a much greater audience. In mid-August of 1969, Yamaha steel-strings would reach the biggest one-day audience to date.

The Bethel, New York, event was called the Woodstock Music and Art Fair. The now-legendary event was unprecedented at the time in terms of its scope and ambition. Over 400,000 people attended, one of whom was a performer named Country Joe McDonald. McDonald was scheduled to play with his band, Country Joe and the Fish, on Sunday, but he went to the stage on Friday to see Richie Havens kick off the festival.

"I was just sitting on the stage grooving, watching Richie Havens," recalls McDonald. "When Havens stopped playing, they asked me if I wanted to do a solo set. I was really nervous about playing by myself in front of that huge crowd, so I started making excuses for why I couldn't do it. I said, 'I don't have a guitar.' That's when someone

The FG500: Yamaha's first solid-top production guitar.

found me that Yamaha. It was an FG150. To this day, I don't know where they got it. It had to belong to someone onstage. I thought to myself, 'Oh, God—they're really going to make me do this.' So I said, 'Well, there's no guitar strap. I can't play without a strap.' So they cut a piece of rope off the rigging, tied it to that Yamaha guitar, and said, 'You're on, pal.'"

McDonald walked onstage and stood in front of two microphones—one for his vocal and one for the FG150—and in front of a vast sea of concertgoers. Despite the relatively primitive mic setup and the fact that the sound people were still dialing the system in after only one performer, McDonald's set sounded surprisingly good. "I thought it sounded like a big coffeehouse," he says. "It's a credit to that Yamaha guitar and to the sound people at Woodstock that that guitar had such presence. You can hear it on the record and in the movie—it sounded really good. And that's not easy, because the FG150 is a small-bodied guitar, and it's got to project out of the soundhole, into the microphone, and out the PA. I was an apprentice at John Lundberg's guitar shop in Berkeley up until my folksinger days. He's a master craftsman, and he taught me a lot about acoustic guitars. Some can project and some are just dead in the water, and that FG150 could project, man."

The Woodstock performance made McDonald a certified folk hero and gave him a special appreciation for the venerable FG150. "I tried to get one a few years ago, and I found that the people who have them won't give them up. I finally got one after a year and a half of looking. It's a great guitar—a wonderful little workhorse. And at the time of Woodstock, that guitar sold for under $100. That's unbelievable. Most guitars in that price range were horrible. I really feel like Richie Havens and I took the acoustic to another level that day at Woodstock—we started a new style of really loud, powerful, rock-and-roll acoustic guitar playing. And my life would have been totally different if they had handed me a typical $100 acoustic. I thank my higher power that they handed me a Yamaha FG150!"

FG75

Yamaha's student-sized FG75.

Now that Yamaha steel-strings were available outside of Japan, word began to spread quickly that there was a well-made, inexpensive alternative to the American acoustics from Martin, Guild, and Gibson. The FG's reach extended to Australia, where a young Frank Gambale discovered them. Gambale would go on to become a jazz-fusion master with the Chick Corea Elektric Band (and have a Yamaha electric bear his name); but at the time, he was a kid just out of high school. "I was eighteen and working in a music store at the mall," he recalls. "The store had these Yamaha FG acoustics that were huge sellers. They cost about $100, looked great, and sounded great. I couldn't keep them in stock." Gambale was impressed not just with the guitars' affordable price point, but with the quality of their construction as well. "They were very solidly made. They had good necks and comfortable action. The quality control was just great. Every time I pulled one out of the box, I had to do nothing. The people at Yamaha really seemed to have their craftsmanship together."

In keeping with the company tradition of continually moving forward with guitar design and improving quality, Yamaha began making solid-top acoustic steel-strings in the late 1960s. Solid—as opposed to laminated—tops are, generally speaking, more desirable in acoustic guitars. A solid top is more resonant and can produce more volume and clarity

FG1500

than a laminated top. The tone of solid-top acoustics will also tend to improve with age, making vintage solid-tops very sought after. The FG500 was the first solid-top model to be produced by Yamaha, and now the late-1960s and early-1970s models command high prices on the collectors' market.

Yamaha had developed a well-deserved reputation for drawing new players to the instrument, and in the late-1960s, introduced the FG75 student guitar. This small-bodied six-string made it easier for young or diminutive players to get around on the guitar. The FG75 was recommended by teachers to beginning guitar students everywhere, and would remain in production for years—becoming a huge success for Yamaha.

The early 1970s saw Yamaha increasing production of handcrafted instruments. The first handmade steel-strings were the FG1500 and FG2000 models. Yamaha again consulted leading acoustic guitarists when designing these instruments, which led to improvements in many areas. The FG1500 featured a solid spruce top and solid jacaranda back and sides in an effort to achieve a better overall tone. This combination of woods, along with Yamaha's improved dovetail neck joint, created a more pleasing balance between the treble and bass frequencies. The FG2000 had the same features with a slightly larger body shape.

Grammy-nominated singer/songwriter Elliott Smith.

Rock legend Bob Seger with his FG1500.

FG2000

James Taylor

After the introduction of the FG2000, Yamaha would enter into an incredible era of high-profile endorsees. Many of the artists who were drawn to Yamaha steel-strings during this time would come to embody acoustic guitar. It was impossible to hear their names without hearing clear, bell-like acoustic tones. James Taylor was certainly one such artist.

By 1973, Taylor had already rung up several hit records and was universally recognized as a tasteful, evocative player. Although he had a collection of production model and custom acoustics, Taylor would regularly call on his Yamaha FG2000 onstage and in the studio.

The model numbers for Yamaha acoustic guitars would undergo a change in the 1970s, with the FG instruments now

One of Yamaha's first L-series acoustics, the L31.

called the "L" series. The acoustics would change structurally as well, with the scale length increasing from 25 inches to 25 9/16. As with the FG bodies, the L acoustics feature a slightly narrower upper bout than a traditional dreadnought shape. Cosmetically, the L guitars were more ornate than the FGs, with abalone and mother-of-pearl inlay on many models.

Another acoustic icon who would join the Yamaha fold around this time was Paul Simon. Simon's acoustic parts were the soundtrack to America's collective identity crisis in the war-torn late 1960s and early 1970s. When Simon received his custom Yamaha L52, he had already penned the Simon & Garfunkel tunes that would make him a legend, and was enjoying a successful solo career. And when his millions of fans would come to see him perform, he'd take the stage with his Yamaha acoustic.

Other members of the L series were the L51, L53, and L54 guitars. Multi-instrumental, cross-cultural genius David Lindley would do great work on his L51 steel-string.

L51   *L52*   *L54*

L5

John Denver

The L53 steel-string became a favorite of John Denver, who ordered two of the acoustics in 1977. Denver's L53 reached a huge audience thanks to the singer/songwriter's prominent concert and television performances. The guitar, built for Denver by Mr. Terry Nakamoto in the Japanese Custom Shop, featured an aged Hokkaido spruce top, Brazilian rosewood back and sides, and intricate inlay on the headstock. It can be seen on the cover of the album *John Denver and the Muppets: A Christmas Together.* Doug Buttleman was running Yamaha's artist relations department in the States at the time, and he recalls Denver's L53. "That acoustic they made for John Denver was one of the best-sounding guitars I've ever heard," he says. "John was a huge proponent of Yamaha acoustics. He was very proud of them and he played them because he honestly felt they were superior in sound and construction."

In addition to these models coming out of the Japanese facility, Yamaha had also been producing guitars in Taiwan since 1972. The guitars made in Taiwan included several affordable, less ornate steel-strings in the L-series line, such as the L5, L6, and L8.

As the decade of the 1970s continued, Yamaha introduced the CJ body shape to its acoustic line. These "Country Jumbo" guitars, which appeared out of the Taiwan facility in 1977, sported a larger body, with a solid spruce top and solid maple back and sides. This construction made for more lows (from the larger body) and more highs (from the maple in the recipe), and produced a tone that many top players were drawn to. The new line included the CJ7, CJ10, and CJ15B, among others.

The CJ52 would be the Yamaha Country Jumbo to attract the biggest names, however. Paul Simon played his custom CJ52 during many of his high-profile gigs. Yamaha offered the XS56E as a production model similar to Simon's CJ52.

CJ15B

John Denver and his custom L53 among friends.

The new CJ, or Country Jumbo, series: the CJ7, CJ10, and CJ15B.

John Lennon's "The Dragon"

The following article was written by Darren Power, Marketing Manager for guitars and drums at Yamaha Kemble in the UK. This story was originally published in *Guitarist* magazine.

The Guitar that John Built

It's a little-known fact that John Lennon and the design team at Yamaha Japan devised and created the most expensive acoustic guitar the custom shop had ever built.

The Yamaha company first came into contact with John Lennon in 1977 when he visited Japan for a holiday with Yoko Ono. It took the Yamaha people by surprise when they heard that the ex-Beatle would like to see them, but, nevertheless, a meeting was organized in a Tokyo hotel.

Apparently, John had played the custom acoustic that Yamaha had made for Paul Simon (the black, abalone-inlaid guitar that can be seen in Simon and Garfunkel's Central Park concert video) and was very impressed. However, John wanted his guitar to have a bigger body and a unique look, so an evaluation session was organized at Yamaha with a selection of stock models. John settled on the CJ52 as the basis for his design as the dimensions were right, and he felt the sound was an improvement on Paul's guitar. This instrument, therefore, was to be the foundation for the project.

As for the unique look, John said to the Yamaha builders in the same meeting: "I love oriental art; is it possible to inlay a dragon using Maki-e?" John drew a rough sketch of what he was looking for there, and then he was very definite as to the importance of this style of work for the guitar and proposed that he would like the Chinese letter for "dragon" on the headstock, also using the Maki-e technique. Lastly, he requested the Tomoe symbol be included behind the bridge; the shaded and light halves of the Tomoe (yin and yang) symbol signify opposites, such as light and dark, good and bad, plus and minus, etc.

After the first evaluation meeting, the Yamaha luthiers went away and studied the Maki-e method, as this type of work had never previously been carried out on guitars or associated with guitar building (and it has not been used since).

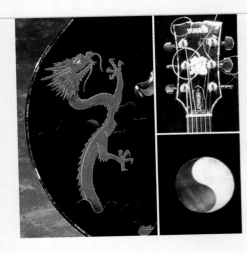

Maki-e is a traditional Japanese decorative art carried out with a natural lacquer extracted from the Urushi tree and colored with the use of gold and silver powder.

The problem with this very traditional style of decorative art was that the work had to be steam kilned in an environment containing more than 90% humidity to enable the natural lacquers to get a good drip on the surface of the guitar. This presented something of a headache for the team, since too much humidity would obviously spoil the wood and build in potential problems for the guitar in years to come.

One week later, John was invited to attend a second meeting, and the construction problems were explained to him. After much discussion, he still wanted to go ahead with his original idea, so Yamaha decided to persevere with the techniques they had already begun to explore. The eventual solution was that the guitar had to be completely finished first—including the inside surfaces, bracing, and kerfing. To add to this, the finish had to be much thicker than usual, and the team realized that such a heavy coating would inhibit the wood's subtle vibrations and so compromise the nuances that make an acoustic guitar sing.

A lengthy trial-and-error process then began to balance the amount of finish the wood could take in order to withstand steam kilning and still sound good. Likewise, tests were done to see what humidity level was needed for the Maki-e technique to take hold. Eventually, a balance was struck, the result being that some low-end projection was sacrificed.

Despite all these difficulties, the finished guitar sounded unique. John was very pleased with the result of everyone's labors, and the Yamaha luthiers were delighted that they had been able to meet the requirements of such a respected and particular customer. This instrument also broke the record for the most expensive Yamaha acoustic guitar ever made—a record that still stands today. And when you bear in mind that these luthiers regularly custom-build acoustic guitars for well over £10,000, it was no mean feat!

Bruce Springsteen

Like a lot of guitar-wielding folk singers, Bruce Springsteen has a profound respect for Bob Dylan. Leading legendary talent scout John Hammond (who discovered both artists) called Springsteen the "new Dylan." And despite his penchant for posing with an electric guitar on album covers, the Boss chose the acoustic guitar to drive many of his tunes.

Staying true to the folk side of his roots, Springsteen released the all-acoustic *Nebraska* in 1982. This was on the heels of his most successful—and primarily electric—album, *The River*. And when one of his most famous songs, "Born in the USA," was misinterpreted and co-opted by political forces, he began performing the song on acoustic guitar to remind people of its original meaning.

All of this makes Springsteen's choice of Yamaha acoustics in the studio and onstage very significant. A brutally honest singer/songwriter, the Boss won't play anything he doesn't believe in.

Bruce, with his trusted CJ52, performing at Madison Square Garden in 1987.

Jimmy Page

With his work with the mighty Led Zeppelin, Jimmy Page set a standard for acoustic textures that has scarcely been equaled. From the DADGAD stylings of "Black Mountain Side" off Zep's landmark 1969 debut to the intricate flat-top work on 1975's *Physical Graffiti*, the acoustic guitar has always been one of Page's most potent sonic weapons. His acoustic parts on *Led Zeppelin III* might be his most influential, with layer upon layer of deep, rich timbres laid down with 6- and 12-string acoustics as well as high-strung or Nashville-tuned guitars.

One of the most legendary guitarists of all time, Page has always had access to whatever gear he needed to get his music across. And, although he has played almost every conceivable make of guitar, he relied on Yamaha acoustics for Zeppelin's 1975 world tour as well as the historic Page/Plant *Unledded* tour in the mid '90s, choosing them for their tone and roadworthiness.

CJ52

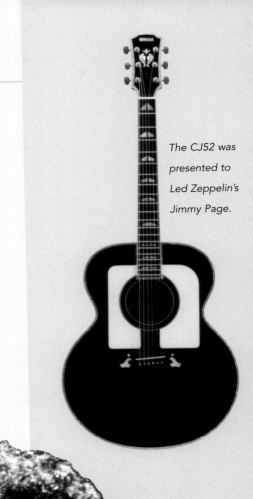

The CJ52 was presented to Led Zeppelin's Jimmy Page.

Jimmy Page plays a Yamaha Jumbo during the Unledded tour in 1998.

The ground-breaking APX10A.

APX Line

The 1980s

The decade of the 1980s signaled many changes for Yamaha's acoustic guitar production. The LS series of small-bodied acoustics was introduced. These instruments had solid tops as well as solid back and sides.

What had been the L series was now known as the "LL" line of guitars, with models such as the LL5, LL25, and LL55. Other introductions to Yamaha's acoustic division included the "LA" or "Luxury Artist" series. The LA57 was a favorite of Kenny Loggins, who was enjoying a huge string of hits at the time.

The introduction of the APX line represented a fairly radical departure from the dreadnought and jumbo designs of the 1970s. The APX10 featured a body that was shallower from front to back, consisting of a spruce top and sycamore back and sides. The woods were not new to Yamaha acoustics, but the look was. For starters, the APX10 featured a cutaway to facilitate upper-fret access. The oval soundhole was another new visual aspect.

But Yamaha had done a clever twist on the concept with the APX. It involved a hexaphonic piezo pickup or, essentially, one pickup per string. A three-position switch enabled the player to send all six strings to a single amp in mono; or, with a two-amp

An early acoustic-electric: the FG350E.

system, send the three treble strings to one amp and the three bass strings to another or send the first, third, and fifth strings to one side and the second, fourth, and sixth strings to the other. The possibilities were mind-boggling.

Guitarist Steve Lukather was an early proponent of the APX10. Lukather, a veteran of a zillion sessions with Michael Jackson, Paul McCartney, Elton John, and many others, was best known for his work with his own Grammy Award-winning band Toto. His incredible range of styles and stunning chops made Lukather an ideal candidate for the innovative APX. "It's a great guitar," he told Yamaha at the time. "What killed me about the guitar was its stereo feature. Not fake stereo. Real. Not done with delays. You play it and it goes left-side, right-side, left-side, right-side." Lukather used the APX10 on Toto's *Fahrenheit* record, tracking the tune "Lea" on it. He also played an extended solo on the accompanying tour on the APX. "It was really cool—I ran it in stereo, bouncing back and forth all over the place."

Susanna Hoffs with the
Bangles playing an APX
acoustic-electric 12-string.

Steve Lukather (right) and Steve Farris
trade licks in an ad for the APX series.

Wynonna Judd

Half of one of the most successful duos in country music history: Wynonna Judd and her APX10.

Suzanne Vega playing acoustic.

Wynonna Judd helped make the APX10 a success by playing it on numerous sold-out shows with her million-selling duo, the Judds. Dealers nationwide couldn't keep the APX in stock after Wynonna showed the guitar off onstage, at the Grammys, and on platinum recordings.

Variations on the APX10 included the APX10T, which sported Indian rosewood back and sides, and the nylon-string APX10N.

On the Road Again

Singer/songwriter Edwin McCain is another APX fan. Since stumbling upon an APX6 in a music store many years ago, he has logged countless hours on that guitar, as well as many other Yamahas.

"That APX6 was just an indestructible guitar," says McCain. "For whatever reason, it seemed made for hard road use. I must have done 1,000 gigs on that thing before I gave it to a friend who plays in Hootie and the Blowfish. He's still got it."

Throughout his career, McCain has been known as a road warrior, touring constantly. The problems he had experienced with guitars breaking down on the road disappeared when he got his Yamaha.

"My primary need in a guitar is durability. You can get into the finer details of the joinery and the cosmetics of an acoustic, but if it only lasts four days on the road before it needs a truss-rod adjustment, that's no good. I need to be able to pull it out

of the case and have it intonate and play in tune. And man…as far as that APX6 is concerned, I don't ever remember adjusting it. It'd go from a sweaty club into a cold trailer, from a hot, humid town to a town where it was snowing, and keep delivering. It's a testament to how well they're made."

Another aspect of the APX6 that appealed to McCain was the flexibility of the guitar's electronics. "The amplified sound of that guitar was really malleable," he says. "Acoustic-electrics are very susceptible to room dynamics and, as those change, the guitar is dealing with a lot of different frequencies. Being able to notch out the pesky ones quickly is key, and you can really do that with this system."

McCain's main acoustic these days is a jumbo-bodied CJX32 that was featured prominently on his *Messenger, The Austin Sessions*, and *Scream & Whisper* albums. "That jumbo is the guitar I go to the most," he says. "I wrote all the songs on my last record on that. Most of the time I record it with a large-diaphragm condenser mic near the soundhole and an AKG pencil mic up near the neck. It's got a pickup in it, but it sounds so good in the room I always try to capture that sound."

A trusty APX10 that McCain converted to Nashville tuning (with the bottom four strings tuned an octave above standard) adds sparkle to many of the tracks.

McCain's loyalty to his Yamaha acoustics also comes from his relationship with the people at the company who have supported his music for years.

"Yamaha's artist support is unrivaled—they're very friendly to the work-ing musician. We've had big ups and big downs, but we've worked consistently. Yamaha has always been there to help us, regardless of chart position."

Centennial Model

Yamaha celebrated a milestone in 1987—100 years as a company. To recognize the momentous occasion, they built a special centennial acoustic with diamonds inlaid on the guitar.

Edwin McCain with his go-to guitar: a CJX32.

The LL100D: Yamaha's 100th Anniversary model.

LL100D

One More from the Road

McCain's experience of the roadworthiness of Yamaha acoustics is not unique. Many players over the years have found that while guitars from many manufacturers drift in and out of tune and in and out of playability, their Yamahas remain consistent. Before Vertical Horizon guitarist Matt Scannell had platinum records up on his wall, he was a struggling musician on the road, logging countless hours of acoustic gigs. His guitar was a Yamaha FG450SA.

"I toured for two years on that Yamaha," says Scannell. "It has a nice, big, round neck that I love. And it was unbelievably solid on the road. I watched a lot of very expensive acoustics from major guitar companies blow up during those tours, and my Yamaha just kept on going."

Scannell would write the bulk of the first two Vertical Horizon albums on his FG450. And he was more than happy to spread the word about the playability and reliability of his Yamaha. "I recommended to a friend that he get one," he recalls. "When I played his, I loved it so much I stole it from him and recorded the first Vertical Horizon album on it."

The FPX

As popular as dreadnought and jumbo-sized guitars are for players who want their big sound for strumming, fingerpickers have always preferred small-bodied acoustics because of their brilliant, delicate, high-end response. Yamaha released a pair of smaller-than-dreadnought acoustics

around the turn of the 21st century—the FPX300 steel-string and FPX300N nylon-string. With their slotted headstocks and slightly wider nuts (1 7/8 inches as opposed to 1 11/16 inches), these instruments were reminiscent of classic fingerstyle guitars. The FPX was a hit with players, and won awards from guitar magazines.

When Steely Dan sideman Jon Herington needed a couple of acoustics for a Bette Midler tour, he was immediately struck by the FPX, which was shown to him by Steely Dan fan and fellow Yamaha user Frank Gambale.

"Frank and I had been playing some Steely Dan tunes, and he showed me this new acoustic he had used on a recent Chick Corea record. He told me he was really impressed with how this FPX guitar had recorded. When I played it, I couldn't believe how well it intonated and how easy it was to play. When I got this Bette Midler tour and I needed a steel-string and a nylon-string, Frank hooked me up with Yamaha, and I got these FPXs."

The FPX acoustics sport solid cedar tops with ovankol back and sides. The electronics package is Yamaha's System 45 two-way system, with a piezo and a soundhole mic on a gooseneck. Herington is particularly pleased with the FPX's amplified tones.

"It's a nice, balanced tone that is really high-volume friendly," he states. "You can play them so loud with no feedback. I use them with a wedge monitor and I've never had any problems. The acoustic tone isn't real boomy—it's got a nice top end—and that might help with feedback. Most amplified acoustics sound horrible to me, but these come off sounding very natural at a high volume. I'm using the steel-string FPX300 on an upcoming Boz Scaggs tour. I haven't heard an amplified acoustic that I like better."

More Unplugged

Yamaha expanded the already-successful LL series to include the LLX6, an acoustic-electric dreadnought model. The LLX6 caught the attention of Jane's Addiction guitarist Dave Navarro. "I'm an electric guy," says Navarro, "but the bands I play in always do an acoustic number. When I saw these guitars, I thought they were great." Although he initially got the LLX6 strictly for amplified live work, Navarro also loved the guitar's acoustic tone. "I have to be concerned with how it's going to sound in the house," he says, "but it sounds amazing acoustically, as well—lots of body and warmth. It used to be that I would have one guitar for live and one to write on. I do both with this guitar."

Because the live capabilities were what attracted him to the LLX6 in the first place, the flexible electronics package in the guitar is a major selling point for Navarro. The combination of a mic and a piezo pickup gives him the control he needs from venue to venue.

"Things always seem to change from sound check to showtime," he says. "When they do, it's nice to have the ability to deal with it. If my guitar is feeding back in the monitor, I don't have to wait for the monitor guy—I can fix it myself.

"And this guitar not only sounds great, it's also really easy to play. I have small hands, so I need a comfortable neck and a nice, light action. Because I'm going from electric to acoustic and back again, I don't want there to be any adjustment. And these acoustics play so smooth and silky, I don't even have to think about it. This neck is perfect for me."

Navarro definitely sees the LLX6 as being a big part of his studio work in addition to the live performances. "There's something magical about putting the sparkle of an acoustic over a rock track," he says. "I love how Led Zeppelin and the Beatles would put those little chimey sounds in the chorus of a song that are almost imperceptible, but if you take them away you miss them. That's how I want to use my Yamaha—to add color and texture to songs and also as the primary instrument on a tune. Plus, I see this acoustic as my main writing guitar. There's just a feeling you get when you write on a great acoustic that doesn't

translate the same way when you play through your electric rig. I can dial in deeper to the soul of the matter when I write on this guitar."

Other additions to Yamaha's acoustic world included the jumbo-bodied LJ16, LJ6, and the acoustic-electric cutaway LJX6C. It was the latter that was the choice of Sevendust guitarist Clint Lowery when it came time to record his band's live acoustic album, *Southside Double-Wide*.

"I was instantly inspired when I got these guitars," says Lowery, who also played an LL16 on the record. "They're really warm, they have a lot of volume, and they play great. I string my electrics pretty heavy, so it wasn't really that much of an adjustment to play these acoustics."

One listen to *Southside Double-Wide* reveals a huge, full acoustic tone with uncommon punch and power. Part of that could be due to Lowery's penchant for heavy strings and tunings as low as low A♯ on his lowest string. "That can be tricky when you're tuned that low," he says. "You have to use a really light touch to play in tune."

Part of the big acoustic sounds on the record came from the fact that Sevendust had removed one of the biggest obstacles for amplified acoustic guitars: feedback from the monitors. "We graduated to in-ear monitors for this tour," explains Lowery. "I tried to amplify acoustics through the wedges before and it never worked right. I'd always get that low feedback. With the in-ears you don't have to worry about that. The soundman can just concentrate on the acoustic's tone in the house and not pull a bunch of frequencies out to help the monitors. I could dial in the pickups in the Yamahas any way I wanted and I was able to get a full, crisp acoustic tone with a lot of low end. That tone—and the ability to hear it so well—made us play tighter, so the overall sound was a lot heavier."

Lowery was happy to get the opportunity to capture his Yamaha acoustics on a live recording that will be around for a long time. "It was challenging to play some of these songs with no gain or effects," he admits. "But when you can get a song over with just an acoustic guitar and a vocal, that's the truest form of a song."

Dave's addiction: Dave Navarro with an LLX6 acoustic-electric.

Sevendust guitarist Clint Lowery.

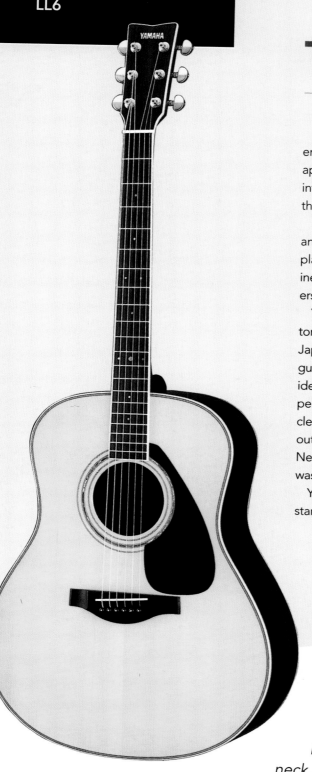

LL6

The New L Series

At the 30th anniversary of Yamaha acoustic guitars, the designers and engineers of Yamaha's guitar team decided that it was time for a new approach to their acoustic guitar. So after a few years of intensive research into the acoustic properties, the structural configuration, and the trends of the acoustic guitar playing community, the New L series was conceived.

Yamaha designers, led by Hiroshi Sakurai, traveled to the United States and Europe to attend the premier gatherings of acoustic guitar makers and players. At the Healdsburg Guitar Festival in northern California, they examined the finest contemporary acoustic instruments, and talked with the players, owners, and builders of them.

Yamaha's guitar team talked with one more group of key people in the history of Yamaha guitars, the Yamaha Custom guitar owners. This group of Japanese players and collectors, who ordered and purchased one-of-a-kind guitars from Yamaha's original Custom Shop, were the first to see the New L idea. They shared their thoughts and visions for what they considered the perfect acoustic guitar. That vision was a guitar that played easily, and had clear balance, significant bottom end, and a treble tone that would stand out. Finally, in July of 2003, around the Nashville Summer NAMM Show, the New L prototypes were shared with many professional players. The response was exciting. With a few adjustments, the guitars were ready for market.

Yamaha has always maintained unique body shapes that resemble industry standards, but remain original to Yamaha. Basically, the New L series has

These photos show the unique construction features of the New L series, including the bracing, five-piece neck, and new C block.

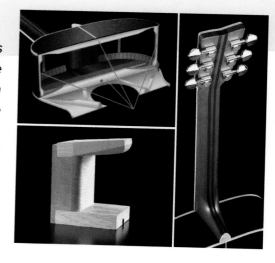

three standard Yamaha body shapes: The LL, which is Yamaha's western body; the LS, which is a deeper body concert configuration; and the LJ, which is more like a grand auditorium.

The specifications include Engelmann spruce tops and rosewood back and sides, and a specially designed, five-piece padauk and mahogany neck. The new sound and feel are generated by a few key elemental changes in construction. The most obvious one is the five-piece neck. By combing the padauk and mahogany with a laminated design, the builders were able to increase the structural integrity of the neck so that it was stronger against any twisting or warping due to environmental changes. The next key point in construction was the "C Block" design used in the neck joint. By incorporating this new block design along with the traditional dovetail joint, it was possible to strengthen the joint, minimize movement in this key area, and also bring together the back of the guitar with the heel area of the instrument. The all-around effect is that the joint is stronger and transmits more of the key vibrations in the most important areas of the guitar's design.

The other point of unique design was the new "Square Frame" and an exact 90-degree X-bracing joint in the crossing point of the top bracing. This new structure has proven to maximize the acoustic resonance and increase the structural integrity of the guitar's body. In the end, the overall instrument is stronger and sounds richer than any other acoustic guitar that Yamaha has ever made.

In a variety of simple, elegant-looking instruments, with prices that make it possible for players of all levels to get their hands on these guitars, the New L series of Yamaha acoustic guitars is Yamaha's greatest acoustic contribution.

LL16

LL36

Compass Readings

The builders at Yamaha increased their acoustic-electric offerings with the beautiful Compass series in 1998. These handcrafted guitars have bodies that are slightly smaller than a full-sized jumbo, and all feature Yamaha's two-way pickup system that combines a soundhole microphone with an under-saddle pickup. In keeping with the navigational theme, Yamaha introduced four models—one for each point of the compass—with unique wood combinations and inlay for each. For instance, the East model features a solid spruce top with quilted mahogany back and sides and an all-seeing eye inlay inspired by ancient Egypt. The North model also has a solid spruce top but with satin sycamore back and sides and an arctic-theme inlay.

The Compass series grew to include several other models in a variety of finishes and wood combinations. The CPX15CM model, with its solid cedar top and mahogany back and sides, has become a favorite of songstress Liz Phair. "I love that guitar," she says. "It really resonates. It's a friendly sounding guitar. That's the guitar I write on at home." Phair's guitarist and musical director Dino Meneghin is also a fan of the Compass and its acoustic-electric capabilities. "Onstage, we use about 25 percent mic and the rest piezo," he says. "It's a great sound."

CPX15NA

Liz Phair with her CPX15CM acoustic-electric.

Other Compass series users include Triumph's Rik Emmett, the Scorpions' Mathias Jabs, SHeDAISY's Kristyn Osborn, and current Dokken 6-stringer Richie Kotzen.

Parlor Music

Another addition to Yamaha's acoustic family comes in a small package. Small, as in the 25-inch scale, parlor-sized, csf steel-string. The CSF60 and CSF60C both feature solid Sitka spruce tops, solid Sapele back and sides, and African mahogany necks. The CSF35 has nato back and sides and a nato neck. The acoustic-electric CSF60C features a sweeping cutaway for increased upper-fret access.

The small body size, slightly shorter 25-inch scale length, and vintage-style open-back tuning machines of the cfs series recall the beloved American parlor guitars from the early 1900s. Super sideman Greg Leisz is an aficionado of those early American acoustics, and he's excited about the CSF line.

CPX15SA

CPX15WA

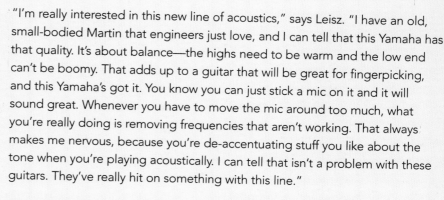

"I'm really interested in this new line of acoustics," says Leisz. "I have an old, small-bodied Martin that engineers just love, and I can tell that this Yamaha has that quality. It's about balance—the highs need to be warm and the low end can't be boomy. That adds up to a guitar that will be great for fingerpicking, and this Yamaha's got it. You know you can just stick a mic on it and it will sound great. Whenever you have to move the mic around too much, what you're really doing is removing frequencies that aren't working. That always makes me nervous, because you're de-accentuating stuff you like about the tone when you're playing acoustically. I can tell that isn't a problem with these guitars. They've really hit on something with this line."

The Sound of Silence

A key to successful acoustic guitar building is respecting tradition. The time-honored designs are as popular as they are for a reason, and guitarists have never been the best when it comes to embracing change. But, if a new design or concept emerges that seems to have the proper balance of old-school reverence and forward-thinking innovation, guitarists will love it. That balance is precisely what Yamaha achieved with the introduction of the Silent Guitar in 2003.

This amazing creation knocked out players and spectators alike with its incredibly lightweight composite body frame that breaks down for easy transportation. The Silent Guitar, available in both nylon- and steel-string models, features a mahogany neck and rosewood fretboard. Players can practice and monitor through headphones—ideal for apartment dwellers, late-night jammers, or anyone prone to getting noise complaints. The custom designed pickup system by L.R. Baggs and B-Band can be further modified by an onboard signal processor for reverb.

Although it might not seem obvious at first glance, Lee Ritenour is the perfect candidate for the Silent Guitar. He was a pioneer of guitar synth playing and is no stranger to new and interesting twists on the 6-string.

"We converted a Yamaha SG solid-body to a synth guitar for 360 Systems back in 1977," says Rit. "I played it on my *Captain Fingers* album. I remember Yamaha's guitar synth that they put out where the strings were just contacts for the frets—that was a wild instrument. So, the concept of the Silent Guitar didn't seem strange to me."

Ritenour first came in contact with the Silent technology through the Silent Bass while on tour in Japan. "Dave Carpenter was on bass with

Lee Ritenour with his SLG100N.

me," he says. "We were playing these big halls and he wanted to use the Silent Bass. The sound was so impressive and it just looked great. When they developed the nylon-string Silent Guitar, I checked it out as soon as I could. When I got one, I plugged it into the board, and it sounded incredible. I think Yamaha may have surprised themselves by how good this thing sounds. I think they designed it for the person on the go—it comes apart and you can pack it up so easily—but I don't know if they thought a bunch of pros were going to be attracted to it for the stage and the recording studio."

Ritenour has gigged all over the world with his SLG100N, and his experience—and the crowd reaction—has been overwhelmingly positive.

"Crowds love this guitar," he says. "It blows people's minds, especially if I break it down onstage. And for me, as a player, I'm really happy with it. The intonation is dead on, which for a classical guitar is not easy. I love the balance of it, too. I thought it might be uncomfortable to play, but it's incredibly comfortable. And it records like a dream. It's on about four cuts on my new DVD *Over Time*, and it sounds great. I definitely see using it more in the studio, as the primary melody or solo instrument on a track. It doesn't replace a classical guitar with a mic on it, but I don't need to replace that. It's got a unique sound; it's its own thing."

The steel-string version of the Silent Guitar is also a head-turner, and it caught the eye of Finger Eleven guitarist James Black. Black took an SLG100S on the road in support of his band's hit song "One Thing," which ended up being a great showcase for his Silent Guitar.

"I use the Silent Guitar for the two songs that were done with acoustics in the studio," says Black, "and that includes 'One Thing.' I like its acoustic tone a lot—really nice and full, and it doesn't feed back. People are always curious about that guitar. They don't know what to make of it because it looks like it's missing big parts, but it sounds really good. I've never had anyone compliment me on my tone when I played a regular acoustic, but people come up all the time and talk about this one. It took a little getting used to, because it doesn't feel exactly like an acoustic—you can't feel it vibrating against your body. But it's lighter, cooler looking, and doesn't give me any feedback problems. Of all my guitars, this is the one everybody asks about."

It's an amazing journey for Yamaha—from humble beginnings making reed organs in 1887 to a huge corporation today. The common thread running throughout this tale is one of music. Yamaha has always been a music company, first and foremost. The company logo with the three tuning forks adorns everything Yamaha makes. And despite the incredible success the company has enjoyed in so many different fields, Yamaha's legacy remains a musical one. Lee Ritenour sums it up eloquently:

"Because Yamaha is the biggest music company in the world, they've had a tremendous impact on players everywhere. Over the years, they've maintained a consistency that is really respected. When you think about how many of their pianos, band instruments, and beginning classical and steel-string acoustics are out there, they've gotten more people playing music than any company in history."

One Silent Thing: Finger Eleven's James Black with his Silent Guitar.

Silence is golden: the SLG100S Silent Guitar.

"I remember when Yamaha brought me the first guitar in 1974.
I was really flattered that they wanted to work with me.

"What was really amazing to me about that guitar was the inlay with
the Buddha. I didn't realize that they were such craftsmen.
So I stayed with them for a long time.

"I salute Yamaha for still caring for me to be a part of it.

"I'm still very impressed with the passion they have to excel in
whatever they set their mind to do. I salute it and I congratulate it.

"Visiting factories is one of the things I like to do. It makes me feel like
I'm 17 years old. Every time I go to the factory and see how they make
guitars, it's really inspiring. These people should know that they bring a
lot of joy.

"Every person that makes a guitar at Yamaha, every hand, every finger
is a part of it. When I grab it, I'm feeling all those people who took the
time to polish it, to shine it, to tune it. All that stuff is part of it. They
need to be validated.

"The guitars are great. You can just about drop a Yamaha guitar out
of a helicopter and it'll stay in tune. The future is bright and positive
for Yamaha.

"Do something from your heart and still be profitable. A win-win.
That's my thing with Yamaha. In music, everyone wins.

"I salute and I thank Yamaha for all the years of supplying me
with guitars and consistency. I couldn't have done it without them.
Yamaha was my first family."

– Carlos Santana

Electric Guitars

The History of Yamaha Guitars

SGV800

In the Beginning

The 1960s represented an incredibly exciting time throughout the world.

There were charming, charismatic leaders, there was talk of travel to outer space, and there was a pervasive sense of hope and optimism. The music of the times reflected that hopeful energy, with rock and roll still in its brash youth. Kids were crazy about the new sounds from Elvis Presley, Buddy Holly, and Bill Haley, with their exhilarating stage presence and loud guitars. But even so, there wasn't a guitar revolution happening. There was no call to arms. Despite the great guitar music being cranked out by Elvis and company, it seemed as if young people were waiting for something—or someone—to push them right over the guitar edge.

In February of 1964, it happened.

When the Beatles performed on the "Ed Sullivan Show" for the first time, it didn't change the world overnight—it changed the world after their very first *chord*. Suddenly, there were electric guitars everywhere. The Lads from Liverpool gave kids on every street corner the confidence to pick up guitars, write songs, and form bands. There has never been anything like it, before or since.

It was in the wake of this mania that Yamaha began making electric guitars in their Hamamatsu facility in 1965. With their

radical curves, extended headstocks, and multiple switches and gadgets, these early models debuted in 1966 and were a hit with kids eager to explore the brave new world of rock. The futuristic vibe of the first Yamaha electrics—guitars that sported names like SG2, SG3, SG5, and SG7—was in keeping with the promise of space travel and the seemingly endless possibilities of the times.

And, while the Beatles—and, a few years later Jimi Hendrix—certainly kicked the guitar craze into high gear, the burgeoning surf guitar movement also put the electric guitar front and center. Countless instrumental hits by bands such as the Ventures and Surfaris featured memorable guitar melodies that were played on Mosrites and Fenders. The bands displayed their instruments prominently on album covers, and the lines and features of those guitars are reflected in the early Yamaha designs, with their roller knobs, vibrato bars, and single-coil pickups. Yamaha catalogs from the era show Japanese bands with SG guitars clearly riding the tsunami of the surf movement. (In the retro revival of the mid 1990s, Yamaha would reissue the venerable SG7 with the moniker "SGV"—"V" standing for "vintage."

Meegs Rascon with an SGV.

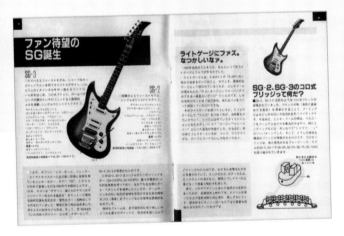

*Pages from an early catalog featuring
the "futuristic" SG models.*

SG7

SGファミリー、
続々と誕生

SG-70
■ナトーボディにマホガニーネックの
重いサウンドが特長。ニューデザイン。
トップはフラット、セットネック。

マイク＝ハンバッキング×2
コントロール＝ボリューム×2、
トーン×2、マイク3W（3点）
ボディ＝ナイン
ネック＝アフリカンマホガニー
ボディ・ネック＝セットネック
重量＝3.8％
カラー＝ナチュラル、レッド
ブラウン、ブラック
発売特標準小売価格→¥60,000（1974年11月）

SG-50
マイク＝ハンバッキング×2
コントロール＝ボリューム×2、
トーン×2、マイク3W（3点）
ボディ＝カツラ
ネック＝アフリカンマホガニー
ボディ・ネック＝セットネック
重量＝3.6％
カラー＝ナチュラル、レッド
ブラウン、ブラック、アイボリーホワイト
発売特標準小売価格→¥50,000（1974年11月）
■カツラのボディにマホガニーネックの
ハイグレード機種。ピックガードのもの
シャープなデザインに、セットネックも特良。

SG使用プレイヤーといえば、まず思い浮かぶの

SG-175
■トップ面がアーチ状になった
便利なデザインを確立。すべて
をハイグレードに、後に登場するオーダーメイドにも。

SG-175スタム本は、
詳価 SG=2000の分体、
マイク＝ハンバッキング×2
コントロール＝ボリューム×2、
トーン×2、マイク3W（3点）
ボディ＝ナンジ＆ラスマホガニー
ネック＝ナンジ＆ラスマホガニー
ボディ・ネック＝セットネック
重量＝3.4％
カラー＝ナチュラル
レッド、ブラウン、ブラック
発売特標準小売価格→¥135,000
（1974年11月）

SG-90
マイク＝ハンバッキング×2
コントロール＝ボリューム×2、
トーン×2、マイク3W（3点）
ボディ＝アフリカンマホガニー
ネック＝アフリカンマホガニー
ボディ・ネック＝セットネック
重量＝3.9％
カラー＝ナチュラル
ブラウン、ブラック
発売特標準小売価格→¥90,000（1974年11月）
■現在のSGと同じアーチ型トップの
デザインを持ったハイグレード機種。
マイク＝カバードタイプのハンバッカー

オーク・ギターにしか採用されなかった貝殻装飾
が、メキシカン・シェルを使ってほどこされて
います。
この SG-175 には翌'75年12月に、オーダーメイ
ドシステムのカスタム・モデルが登場。どちらか
といえば海外ミュージシャンの評価が高かったS
Gですが、このカスタム・モデル発売によって日
本のプロ、セミプロ、アマチュアと、幅広いファ
ン層の人気を得るようになりました。

はカルロス・サンタナ。彼の特注もて仏陀や天女の
インレイを施された SG-175、SG-2000 はあまり
にも有名です。サンタナの他にも、マーク・ファ
ーナー（G・F・R）、ジョージ・テリー（エリッ
ク・クラプトン・バンド）、ヤン・アッカーマン
（フォーカス）、ウィッシュボーン・アッシュ、
渋染龍など、多くの一流ギタリストたちが SG で
プレイしていました。

The SG175 signaled the start of something big for Yamaha guitars.

SG45

Meanwhile, another musical trend was shaping playing styles and instrument production. The folk movement of the 1960s, with its heroes Bob Dylan, Arlo Guthrie, and Simon & Garfunkel, brought tons of players to the acoustic guitar; and Yamaha's acoustic division reaped the benefits. But electric players were also influenced by the folkies, and put their own spin on things with new sounds and instruments. The Beatles and the Byrds were playing an exciting brand of folk music—this time on electric 12-string guitars. Well aware of this trend, Yamaha debuted their first electric 12-string, the SG12A, in 1967. The SG12A featured the same cool lines and single-coil pickups as its 6-string siblings, the SG5 and SG7, but with an expanded, more symmetrical headstock to accommodate the additional six tuning machines.

The 1970s

The decade of the 1970s brought with it an end to Beatlemania and the surf scene, and ushered in a new era of arena mega-rock. Bands like Led Zeppelin and the Who were filling stadiums with loud, crushing rock tones. The twang of the surf bands and the chime of the Beatles' sound had been replaced with thick, powerful tones that were typically created with humbucker-equipped solidbodies plugged into huge stacks of amps. These player preferences showed up in Yamaha's early-1970s creations.

With their dual humbucking pickups, single cutaways, and three-to-a-side tuning machines, Yamaha's SG40 and SG45 models were clearly on track with the popular trends when they were released in 1972. These guitars displayed the quality control and features that Yamaha electrics were beginning to be known for, but they didn't catch on with a prominent player in order to drive sales.

That would all change with the addition of a double-cutaway SG model.

The SG175 was conceived in 1974, and the first production models appeared approximately one year later. The body was made of a relatively thick slab of mahogany that had more in common with the Les Paul than the Gibson SG (the latter of which would later necessitate a name change for Yamaha in the mid 1980s, with instruments sold in the U.S. being labeled "SBG").

While some early Yamaha SG models featured bolt-on and set-neck designs, the neck-through SG2000 would arrive on the scene in 1976 and give Yamaha the dose of star power the company had been waiting for.

When Carlos Santana was first contacted by Yamaha in the mid 1970s, he wasn't won over initially by what he saw in the guitars. Posing on the cover with his Yamaha, he told *Guitar Player* magazine in June of 1978 that the first models he saw were too light, the frets were too thin, and the guitars wouldn't sustain. "I sat down with them," he told *GP*, "and said, 'Look, I can't play the guitar, man. But if you make it more solid, and put more wood on it . . .' For sustain, I asked them to put a big chunk of metal right where the tailpiece is. You hit it and it's like hitting a grand piano—it really resonates. It weighs a lot, but when you hit a note, you don't have to use all those gadgets to sustain."

Santana with one of his Yamaha SGs on the cover of Guitar Player magazine, June 1978.

SG12a

SG40

Carlos on tour in the 1970s
with his SG2000.

After several tries, the SG2000 that Santana and Yamaha settled on was characterized by impeccable craftsmanship, attention to detail, and playability. The fine woods, neck-through construction, and unique, sustain-enhancing features finally gave Santana the guitar voice that he had heard in his head but had struggled to achieve. These unique features—for which Yamaha would receive a U.S. patent—were called the "T-Cross System" and "Sustain Plate." The T-Cross is essentially two flanks of mahogany running along the maple neck, which increased stability and contributed to tone and resonance. The Sustain Plate is a brass plate that is coupled to the Tune-o-Matic-style bridge and mounted under the top.

The use of brass hardware to increase sustain became a common practice in the 1970s; and although players and builders have debated the merits ever since, the combination really worked on the SG2000.

Guitarist Chris Solberg joined Santana in 1978, and played and co-wrote songs on the hit albums *Inner Secrets, Marathon, Zebop!,* and *Shango.* "Carlos's rig at the time," remembers Solberg, "was his blonde Boogie, with the single Altec 12-inch speaker, and the Yamaha SG2000. I played his Yamaha, and it was set up for really low, light action. Carlos was stringing it with .008s. He would play my Strat that had .010s and call them 'telephone poles.'" Solberg remembers Santana being very pleased with the tone and performance of the SG2000 at the time. "The sustain was really important to him. His criteria at the time was that long note in 'Europa.' If he could get that note to really sing, he was happy. And the Yamaha could do it. I think that sustain block had a lot to do with it. My understanding was that Carlos wasn't satisfied with the Yamahas until they put that brass block in there; but after that, he wouldn't play anything else. He played my '55 hardtail Strat on the solo to 'Winning,' but I think everything else he recorded while I was in the band was done with his Yamaha."

The timing couldn't have been better for Yamaha to release such a fine instrument with forward-thinking features and meticulous setup as exhibited on the SG2000. Despite their apparent stranglehold on the guitar market, the

A page out of a Yamaha catalog showing some of the SG features.

Carlos Santana with tennis champ John McEnroe at a New York City concert in the mid '70s.

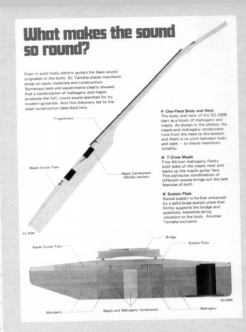

American builders were developing a reputation for resting on their laurels, which resulted in quality control issues. Guitarists were increasingly getting the feeling that they were paying for a famous brand name without the famous quality behind it. Yamaha's Ken Dapron remembers that era well. "Yamaha was already established in the acoustic market in the States," he says. "But what we did with the electrics was, instead of coming out with budget models as we had with the acoustics, we started with the top of the line. The message that Yamaha sent by coming out with the SG2000, the SA2000, and our first basses was that these were high-end instruments for pro players."

A cross-section view of some of the SG2000's unique features, including "T-Cross System" U.S. patent.

SG1000

SG700

SG500

Bob Marley

Is this love? Bob Marley with his SG2000.

Flock of Seagulls guitarist Paul Reynolds, playing an SG model.

SGギタリスト名鑑

Al McCay, Bob Marley, Brian Robertson, Carlos Rios, Carlos Santana, George Johnson, Issei Noro, Johnny Graham.

The same players who might have been hesitant to check out an import in the past were now definitely willing to give Yamaha a try, and were pleased to find a guitar maker who seemed to care about their needs. Santana was one such player. "They go out of their way to make good instruments," he said in the same *GP* story. "The reason I left Gibson was because I feel like they're like McDonald's now. They just wrap a hamburger and throw it at you. There's nothing individual about it. Whereas, Yamaha, to me, is more like my wife at Thanksgiving: She puts effort and time and love behind it and you can feel it. You can feel it when you pick up that guitar." Ironically, it was some of these same Yamaha guitars that would spawn the much-publicized renaissance of the vaunted American guitar manufacturers. And, of course, fans of Santana hits such as "Open Invitation" and "All I Ever Wanted" would do anything to get a piece of his singing, sustaining guitar magic.

By this time, the SG line had grown to include several models with varying features and price points. The SG1000, released in 1976, and the SG800 from 1978 sported Yamaha's "Bi-Sound" circuit, which allowed the player to split the humbuckers' coils with Yamaha's proprietary push/push switches on the tone knobs. This provided the thinner, brighter tones that were popular with funk and blues players. The SG1000-24 (1983) had a 24-fret neck, giving players unprecedented access to the dog-killing upper-register frequencies they craved.

The Yamaha SG line of guitars would go on to become a favorite of players from every style of music. Rocker Dave Meniketti from the band Y&T would use an SG2000 to crank out his brand of melodic hard rock in the 1980s. Fusion master Chris Poland—guitarist with Megadeth and currently with Ohm—credits a mid-1980s SBG1300TS with getting him started on his tone quest.

"I had been playing these high-end guitars that I had spent all this money on, and this Yamaha sounded better than any of them," he says. "I ended up selling my other guitars and getting a backup 1300. After that I started seeking out other Yamahas. Now I've got an SBG2000 and that's just a great all-around guitar for me."

Junsi Yamagishi, Kerry Livgren, Masayoshi Takanaka, Mick Jones, Paul Barrere,

Phil Manzanera, Steve Cropper, Yoshiaki Masuo.

Part of the reason these SGs made such a splash was Yamaha's focus on quality control that continues to this day. In the 1970s, it was very uncommon to properly set up instruments before they went to the dealers. "We were one of the first companies to take Japanese guitars when they arrived and work on them over here in the States," says Ken Dapron. "We would unbox them, let them acclimate in the warehouse for five weeks, level and dress the frets, buff the fingerboards and frets to look like glass, and then restring, set them up, and rub out the finishes before they went to stores. We'd sign and date the inspection card, so if there ever was a problem, you could talk to the original QC inspector. Often, the dealers would call us and say something like, 'When I opened the case, I was stunned by the beauty, craftsmanship, and the way it felt and played.' It was that quality control that helped us win a lot of hook space in stores at a time when Gibson was king."

Thanks in part to the Santana connection, and also to the setup skills of the Yamaha U.S. team, word spread quickly through the guitar community that there was a higher standard in electric guitar craft. Soon, top players could be seen with Yamaha SG models onstage and in studios all over the world. Stax/Volt legend Steve Cropper; Thin Lizzy's Brian Robertson; Earth, Wind & Fire's Al McCay; and reggae god Bob Marley were all delivering memorable music—and selling millions or records—with their Yamahas. "During the R&B and fusion days," says Dapron, "Yamaha SGs found their way into the hands of John McLaughlin, Robben Ford, Larry Carlton, the Jackson 5, and Carlos Rios. The SG2000 was a huge milestone for Yamaha."

The success of the SG line didn't carry over to every part of the Yamaha line in the 1970s, however. Other interesting—but less popular—creations included the SF series from 1977. These were single- and double-humbucker loaded 6-strings that, visually speaking, were somewhere in between the SGs and the Stratoid SC guitars. Another intriguing design that went almost totally unnoticed in the American market was Yamaha's mid-1970s SX series. These bizarre beauties appeared for a two-year period in the mid 1970s, and resembled the mutant offspring of a bouzouki. The devilishly pointed horns of the headstock

Robben Ford

Robben Ford gets into it with his SG2000.

Guitarist Andy Taylor of Duran Duran onstage playing an SG model.

An under-appreciated classic: Yamaha's SX900A.

echoed the sharp, right-angled cutaways of the bodies that must have provided unfettered access to the upper frets for the few players lucky enough to get their hands on these rare birds.

Single-Coils

Although the folks at Yamaha were no longer concentrating on their single-coil-equipped SG2s and 3s by the mid 1970s, they had by no means abandoned that sound. The aforementioned SC line, which appeared in 1977, put a fresh, customized spin on the three-pickup solidbody concept.

The SC700, 800, 1000, and 1200 all featured the offset horns, six-to-a-side tuning machines, and three single-coils that had been mainstays of the Fender Stratocaster for more than twenty years. Where these SC guitars differed, however, was in their unique switching system. Rather than the typical five-way switch, the SCs used individual on/off switches for each pickup, giving guitarists a range of sounds that wasn't possible with the conventional switching system. The additional pickup combinations—all three at once and bridge and neck together—were instantly popular with players looking for new sounds. (This range of tonal options, along with the ability to reverse the phase of the pickups, is what inspired the name of the series, SC: "Super Combination.") In the decade that followed, the guitar world would see a ton of custom builders adopt similar wiring schemes, and many players would have their existing guitars modified to obtain those sounds.

SC1200   *SC1000*   *SC80*

The Dawn of the '80s

The tail end of the 1970s seemed at first glance to be a bad time for the guitar.

Untimely deaths spelled the end or at least drastic changes to the bands that had ruled for years. Disco was king and guitar solos were considered a thing of the past. (Ironically, many rockers were screaming "Disco sucks!" so loudly for so long that they missed out on a lot of great guitar in those dance tunes.) The increased influence of synthesizers in music had many critics writing the guitar's obituary.

Then a band out of Pasadena, California—and their fiery guitarist in particular—single-handedly changed all that. When Edward Van Halen burst on the scene in 1978, he not only forever changed the way the guitar was played, but he also changed the way it looked, the way it sounded, and how it was marketed and sold. The guitar that Van Halen played on his debut album, the one that launched a million finger-tappers and inspired a million copies, was a double-cutaway, single-humbucker, trem-equipped solidbody with outrageous striped graphics. It's safe to say that there wasn't a guitar maker on the planet who didn't change some aspect of their instruments in response to the VH juggernaut that was taking the 6-string world by storm. By 1980, Yamaha's line reflected this new world order of the guitar with the SF3000—a single-humbucker, whammy-bar model.

The Jacksons

The Jacksons onstage.

Tito Jackson with MJ in the mid '80s.

As the 1980s continued, the VH-inspired trend in guitar making evolved. Headstocks got pointier, necks got flatter and wider, and paint and graphics got wilder. But it was the tremolo bridge—now ubiquitous on rock guitars—that underwent the biggest change of all. The double-locking whammy, first brought to prominence by Floyd Rose and popularized by Mr. Van Halen once again, became the most sought-after piece of hardware for guitar. The extreme dive-bombs and other whammy bar tricks were making it difficult to keep guitars in tune. By clamping or "locking" the strings at the two most crucial areas for intonation—the nut and the tailpiece—double-locking systems allowed players to dump the strings down until they went slack, yank them as much as a fifth above standard pitch, and come back perfectly in tune. Every time.

By 1987, Yamaha had their own version of these double-locking shred machines: the RGX series. Built in the Taiwan factory with all-new colors, active electronics, and Yamaha's version of the insanely popular locking whammy bar, the RGX guitars were a huge hit with hard rockers. Our Lady Peace guitarist Steve Mazur remembers getting an RGX112 as his first electric. "It had one humbucker and two single-coils," says Mazur. "I still have that guitar."

Many RGX guitars—such as the RGX1212A—combined features that

RGX220

RGX112

RGX612A

RGX812

were difficult to find in one guitar, like 24-fret, through-body necks, 24 3/4-inch scale lengths, individual on/off switches for each pickup, and ebony fingerboards.

In time, the RGX family would grow to include the piezo-equipped RGX820Z and the 620Z. These instruments reinforced Yamaha's growing reputation as a cutting-edge guitar company for serious players. In 1988, the Image series of guitars was created in collaboration with British guitar designer Martyn Booth. Three models were unveiled: the Custom, the Deluxe, and the Standard. The Image Custom was an arched top double cutaway with two pickups that incorporated Yamaha's H.I.P.S. (Hybrid Integrated Pickup System) technology. This system provided a much wider tonal palette by allowing players to change from humbuckers to single-coils (as well as from active to passive) by flicking a switch. The Custom also included Yamaha's Vintage Pro Tremolo system—with roller bearings and locking tuners—as well as a recessed output jack.

The Image Deluxe and Standard sported archtop bodies and passive electronics.

The end of the 1980s would culminate in the dawn of a new era for Yamaha—a whole new game plan that would carry Yamaha electric guitars into the twenty-first century.

Image Series

Custom

Deluxe

Standard

Michael Lee Firkins

YGD

Yamaha Guitar Development in North Hollywood, California

Yamaha's increased ability to listen to players' needs, combined with their already stellar reputation for quality control, was getting the company noticed by more and more top guitarists. It was natural then, in 1989, to establish a player-friendly home base located in the heart of the music business to interface with these musicians more easily. That home base was Yamaha Guitar Development in North Hollywood, California. YGD could not only modify and customize existing Yamaha designs, but could also create all-new models and prototypes. This hands-on approach was a crucial step in connecting with players, producers, and recording studios in the area.

The first designs to come out of YGD were the Pacifica and the Weddington series. The Weddington was named after the street on which YGD is located. Weddingtons were single-cutaway solidbodies with two pickups—a time-honored design, to be sure, but with plenty of new ideas to set the instruments apart.

Models such as the Weddington Custom had thick, mahogany bodies with flamed-maple tops. The Custom's electronics consisted of two DiMarzio humbuckers and a special four-pole, five-way switch, providing not only the three classic sounds associated with two-humbucker guitars, but also two additional tones unique to Yamaha. Those tones were the result of the neck pickup's coils in parallel (as opposed to in series), and a funky setting that incorporated the inside coils of both pickups wired in series and the remaining bridge pickup coil in parallel and out of phase.

The lobby at YGD.

The Weddington Special featured an all-mahogany body, two DiMarzio Q-100, P-90-style pickups, and an adjustable one-piece bridge/tailpiece. It sported the same sexy lines and deep cutaway that made the Custom so easy on the eyes and hands. And, like the Custom, the Special appealed to players who wanted a classic solidbody look and vibe, but with greater tonal flexibility, attention to detail, and improved ergonomics. Despite this collection of features and attributes, the Weddington lasted only a few years before being discontinued.

At the same time, YGD was working on a design that would prove incredibly successful for Yamaha—the Pacifica. The Pacifica series represented a quantum leap for YGD and Yamaha in general—in that it was an instrument designed and prototyped in the American custom shop with direct input from pro players.

Early Pacifica models such as the 812, 821, and 904 could be seen onstage in the hands of monster players like Ernie Isley, Marc Bonilla, and Michael Lee Firkins. These double-cutaway guitars were regarded amongst serious players as some of the finest of the wave of Super Strat-style guitars on the market. Pacificas sported fast, satin-finish necks (made in America by Warmoth Guitar Products with compound radius fingerboards) and sleek bodies with flawless, mirror-like finishes. They had great-sounding DiMarzio or Seymour Duncan pickups, in the popular hum-sing-sing (one humbucker, two single-coil) and hum-sing-hum configurations. And, with players still wanting whammy bars that wouldn't throw their guitar out of tune, many Pacificas came stock with Floyd Rose systems or the cutting-edge combination of a Wilkinson trem with Sperzel locking tuners. All these features added up to an instrument that could cover a tremendous amount of musical ground. Although many of these trends and design elements were driven by the rock market, players of all stripes were gravitating to the Pacifica, including Carlos Rios; Earth, Wind & Fire's Sheldon Reynolds; and Johnny Cash sideman Kerry Marx. The Pacifica was a huge milestone and one of Yamaha's best sellers.

The dream becomes a reality. A Weddington Custom prototype with highly figured maple top.

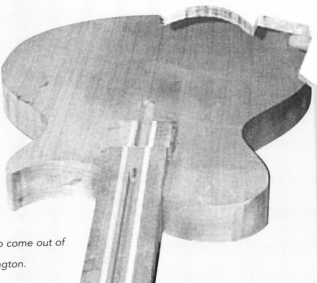

The first design to come out of YGD: the Weddington.

Pacifica

The Pacifica line would grow to include other designs, such as the Pacifica USA1 and USA2, released in 1995. These two solidbodies once again combined popular elements that weren't readily available in a stock guitar.

These beauties were the first and only Yamaha guitars manufactured entirely in the U.S. The USA1 melded a bunch of cool features that added up to a three-pickup guitar (with a bridge humbucker) that provided an incredibly musical array of tones that could cover rock, blues, country, and more. The ingenious switching was made possible by a specially designed four-pole, five-way switch that didn't even exist until Yamaha requested it from one of their switch manufacturers. The maple-capped body added zing and focus to the USA1's voice, and the Wilkinson trem and Sperzel Tremlok tuners made for stable tuning while maintaining a vintage look and feel.

Yamaha was gaining a reputation as a unique, vibrant guitar maker. To cement that image, YGD sought out unique, exciting players in a variety of styles as ambassadors for these new instruments. King's X guitarist Ty Tabor was becoming something of a cult hero in the six-string community for his uncanny sense of melody, amazing tone, and jaw-dropping chops. Tabor first became aware of Yamaha guitars in the mid 1970s, when he played an SG model in a music store.

"I had just gotten a 1976 Les Paul Custom, which was a dream of mine," he recalls. "I wanted to see how the Yamaha compared to my Gibson. I really liked the Yamaha—I thought it was a great guitar.

"YGD made me several Yamahas that I played in the early King's X days. I really liked them, but we didn't do an official deal. It was more of a handshake thing at first." The official deal would go down in the mid 1990s, when Tabor began collaborating with Yamaha on his signature model. He was already pleased with Yamaha's ability to listen to and meet players' needs, and was excited about the possibilities of this new guitar.

"I wanted a guitar that had all the features I couldn't find in one instrument," he explains. "One obvious thing I wanted to improve was the ergonomics—especially for playing live. I don't think guitars were ever designed for live

The single-cutaway Pacifica USA1 and the Pacifica USA2.

playing. They've always been designed for sitting in a chair and playing. The way your arm lays across the top of a guitar affects how you play it, and the sharp edge on a guitar like a Les Paul, for instance, forces me to play in what I consider an unnatural position. So the first thing we did was to take the RGX body style and round off that edge. My arm falls across it really naturally."

As a player who seems to gig every day of his life, Tabor wanted other stage-friendly changes to his instrument. To facilitate seeing the fret markers on dark stages, Tabor had Yamaha inlay markers across the back of the neck. "Markers on the front of the neck don't do me any good," he says. "I can see these much better. Lighting systems don't ever wash them out. That might seem like a minor point, but Yamaha took it seriously. I love that."

The improvements didn't stop with cosmetics and ergonomics, however. To accommodate the full range of Tabor's playing, YGD would also change a fundamental aspect of the guitar's design, and the Drop 6 was born. Detuning is commonplace now, but King's X was tuning low before practically anyone and, with a normal 24 3/4-inch or 25 1/2-inch scale length, it can be difficult to get a low-tuned guitar to intonate and react properly. One way of working around this is to add a low seventh string to the guitar. That was never a consideration for Tabor's signature model. "I've never been one to play seven-strings," he says. "It gets in the way when I'm playing rhythm and palm muting. But even more than that, it doesn't change the voicing of the guitar at all if you're not on that seventh string. Everything else you play just sounds the same."

Enter the Drop 6. The idea was to lengthen the neck to 26 1/4 inches, which would better handle the heavier string gauges for low tunings. Tabor was hooked instantly. "I thought it was a genius idea. The entire sound is completely different, but you can use all your same chord shapes. It feels like a regular guitar even though you're tuned gutter low. The very first Ty Tabor model they made for me was a Drop 6 and then we made a regular scale version as well." Yamaha was the first company to produce a semi-baritone guitar (which is what the Drop 6 is) and many other companies followed suit.

King's X guitarist Ty Tabor, with his Drop 6 model.

The Drop 6 Ty Tabor model.

Frank Gambale

Frank Gambale and the AES FG.

AES Solidbo

A few years later, Yamaha was approached by guitar master Frank Gambale with the idea of creating a signature model. Gambale, a gifted player whose credits include stints with Chick Corea, Vital Information, and many solo and clinic tours, had very definite ideas about what he needed in a guitar. "I first came to Yamaha professionally through my friend Rich Lasner, who helped design the Pacifica," says Gambale. "The Pacifica series really proved that Yamaha could make a great modern guitar." Gambale had long been an admirer of Yamaha pianos and acoustic guitars, and wasn't surprised to find comparable workmanship from YGD. "It made sense that their electrics would follow suit," he says. "High-quality, uncompromising instruments."

Gambale was instantly pleased with his working relationship with Yamaha. "We all got along great, and they were definitely open to creating a model for me." That was the impetus for Gambale's signature guitar—the AES FG.

"The thing about this guitar is it's an original creation—from scratch," he says. "It was a complex process because I had a lot of requests."

Gambale's requests included full access to the upper frets, a bolt-on neck, and rear-mounted pickups. The bolt-on neck question was answered with the advent of Yamaha's Rear Mountable Neck Joint, which provides support without hindering upper-range playability. The FG's whammy system is a Wilkinson VS100, one of the more popular post-Floyd designs. The addition of a trem system led to an unexpected structural and timbral change to the guitar. Gambale explains: "We happened upon this creative thing by accident. When it came time to attach the trem springs to the body, there was no body inside to attach it to, because we had rear-mounted the pickups. So, we ended up attaching the springs to the end of the neck. The amazing resonance that resulted from that coupling was really obvious the first time I played it. It creates this vibration with lots of highs and incredible sustain."

Gambale's tenure with Yamaha seems to be constantly bearing fruit, with album releases and tours happening constantly. A lifelong teacher, Gambale continues to conduct instructional clinics, and even that part of his career is flourishing like never before. "I did a clinic tour in Asia," he says. "I had never been to Bangkok, and when I got there, I found that 1,800 people had shown up for this Yamaha clinic. I had never seen anything like it. There were giant screens on either side of me, and cameras pointed at my hands and face. It was like a giant rock concert with just me onstage. It was freaky, but it shows great interest in the instrument."

The AES line would also be successful for Yamaha, with players from all genres drawn to the solidbodies' sleek lines, rock-solid construction, and great tones. The AES500 and 800 debuted in 1998.

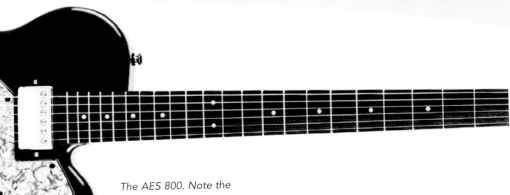
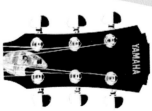

The AES 800. Note the five-way pickup selector.

*Our Lady Peace
guitarist Steve Mazur.*

These guitars sported bolt-on necks and either a nato (500) or mahogany-capped alder (800) body. The 500 was a straight-ahead, two-humbucker model with a three-way switch. The 800 took things up a notch with its DiMarzio DLX Plus or "Q-100" pickups—humbuckers reminiscent of P-90s—and its ingenious switching system that combined the four-pole, five-way switch with a variable phase knob. Early proponents of the AES800 include Black Eyed Peas guitarist George Pajon, Jr. and k.d. lang sideman extraordinaire Greg Leisz. "I brought two AES 800s on a k.d. lang tour," says Leisz. "One was a Drop 6 that I used as a baritone guitar. It has a piezo bridge and I would blend in some of that tone with the other pickups. That guitar is on the song 'Summerfling' from k.d.'s live album."

The AES line would grow to include the 420, 620, and 720—which are produced in the Korean factory—and the current flagship model 920, from Japan.

These are all single-cutaway, set-neck 6-strings with two humbuckers, and all but the 420 sport Yamaha's unique "fingered" tailpiece design—an elegant means of insuring proper string angle and through-body tension across the bridge. Ohm guitarist Chris Poland became an instant fan of the AES series: "I have an 800, and now I'm playing a 620, but those are all great guitars. I did a video for the Yamaha website demonstrating all the AES models, and every guitar they handed me was just a stock guitar, right off the rack. I was struck by how well they all played and intonated—just amazing."

AES420

AES620

Steve Mazur, from the band Our Lady Peace, is another AES convert. "I'm basically a Tele guy," says Mazur, "but I had been playing Les Pauls to get a more powerful sound. When I tried the AES 620, it seemed like the perfect middle ground between a Les Paul and a Telecaster. It had all the power of a Les Paul but with the snappiness and quick response you get from a Telecaster. I love it."

Yamaha's AES series would give rise to two more cutting-edge signature models for Orgy guitarists Amir Derakh and Ryan Shuck. The AES-AD6 is a member of the Drop 6 family, with a 26 1/4-inch scale length to better accommodate Orgy's low tunings. "It was a custom Drop 6 that got me interested in working with Yamaha," explains Derakh. "The longer scale length makes for better string tension since we're tuning down to B. I play a lot of guitar synth, and so that extra tension helps with the tracking."

For Derakh's bandmate, 7-stringer Ryan Shuck, Yamaha created their first ever 7-string model, the AES-RS7. "We had recorded with a few other 7-strings, but we were never really happy with the way they sounded," says Derakh. "When we were working on my guitar we said, 'Hey… Yamaha doesn't have a 7-string. Why don't we do one with this longer scale length?' It worked. This is the best production 7-string I've ever heard, and Ryan uses it exclusively."

Ohm guitarist Chris Poland with his AES 720.

AES720   *AES920*

Stern Lessons

PAC1511MS

Jazz guitarists, like almost all guitarists, are traditionalists. As free as they are when it comes to improvising over changes, they adhere to a fairly strict set of rules when it comes to gear and tone. These rules, unknowingly written many years ago by Charlie Christian and Wes Montgomery, clearly state that jazz should be played on hollowbody guitars with a clean tone and flatwound strings. One guy who never got that memo is Mike Stern. A veteran of Miles Davis' band, Stern bucked the hollowbody trend by dishing out his amazing jazz licks on a solidbody, and a country-approved Fender Telecaster to boot. Indeed, it was impossible to picture Stern without also picturing his humbucker-loaded, natural-finish ash weapon. Which makes his eventual relationship with Yamaha all the more remarkable, culminating in the release of the PAC1511MS.

"Yamaha asked me to check out some stuff years ago," says Stern. "But I was kind of glued to this Tele. See, I bought my original Tele from Danny Gatton, who got it from Roy Buchanan. That one got stolen at a bus station—a cat pulled a gun on me, so he had a pretty persuasive argument! A guy in Boston heard that story and he made me a mutt Tele to replace it. It has a Fender neck, but that's about it. The body is something else and the pickups are a Duncan JB in the neck and, I think, a Barden in the bridge. I used that guitar on my album *Upside Downside* and everything else for years."

Yamaha approached Stern again in the late 1990s with the idea of building a better "mutt." YGD duplicated the dimensions of the neck and the exact placement of the pickups. Because Stern was so comfortable with his old guitar, Yamaha also concentrated on achieving the exact same weight with the new model.

"The first guitars they sent me were close," says Stern, "but I wanted a few changes. I'm not a guitar builder, so I just tell them in basic terms—I either dig it or I don't. I was working with Gotoh in Japan, so I would have a friend who speaks Japanese translate for me when I would get the guitars. After about five tries, they sent me a fantastic instrument."

The Stern model differs slightly from his mutt. The neck pickup is now a Seymour Duncan '59, and the bridge is a Duncan Hot Rails. There are some cosmetic differences but, all in all, Stern is very happy with his new instrument. "I'm kind of a one-guitar guy," he says. "There's just something about an old guitar that I like, so when I got my Yamaha, I wasn't totally comfortable with it at first. But they told me, 'Just keep playing it—break it in.' So I did, and now this thing plays like it's old. The difference in tone is subtle, but I think the Yamaha has more presence and a little more clarity than my mutt. I use it almost exclusively now. It's on my albums *Play*, *Voices*, and *These Times*, and it recorded like a dream. My friends who I've played with for years will come up and say, 'Where's your Tele?' I tell them I'm playing this now. I ask them what they think of the sound and they all love it."

Stern's friends aren't the only ones who love the 1511MS. Steve Mazur is another fan. "I love that Mike Stern guitar," he enthuses. "I end up doing a lot of writing on that guitar. Live, I'll tune it down to C and it just sounds great." Jon Herington, veteran sideman with Steely Dan, Bette Midler, and Mike Stern, employs a 1511MS and, interestingly, tunes it low as well. "I needed a baritone guitar for a Bette Midler tour," he explains. "My tech set up a Mike Stern model to be tuned B to B, and it sounds just amazing. It's fat but not dark-sounding, and that Tele-style bridge pickup is just perfect for baritone. It really cuts."

Stern remains very pleased with not only his guitar, but also his relationship with Yamaha. "Meeting people like Gotoh and then going to the shop in Japan and seeing how they make the instruments was an eye-opener," he says. "My guitar has sold well—especially in Europe—and I'm really flattered by that. This is not an easy business, but these guys at Yamaha really care and people appreciate that."

Mike Stern

"I'm kind of a one-guitar guy," says Mike Stern, pictured here with his signature PAC1511MS.

"I only travel with my Yamahas. They're easy to play and they sound consistantly good, no matter where I'm playing. I know that sounds like an ad, but it's true. That's why I play them."

– Martin Taylor

Archtop/Semi-Hollowbody Guitars

The History of Yamaha Guitars

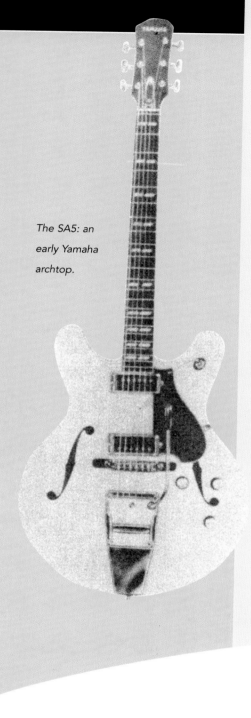

The SA5: an early Yamaha archtop.

Archtops

By the time Yamaha began producing hollow and semi-hollowbody archtop electrics, that style of guitar construction was already very popular with jazz, early rock, and rockabilly players. Combining the familiar look of an acoustic guitar with the still-new and exciting capabilities of electric guitar, these instruments were intriguing and beautiful. And while archtop electrics were featured prominently with rock-and-rollers like Chuck Berry and Elvis guitarist Scotty Moore, these guitars found the most favor with jazz players. Thanks to Charlie Christian, Wes Montgomery, Joe Pass, and many others, big-bodied archtops became the industry standard for playing jazz—and the guitars' warm, round tones defined an entire movement.

The earliest Yamaha archtop, the SA5, was released in 1966, shortly after electric guitar production began at the Japanese factory. American manufacturers dominated the archtop market at the time, and Gibson was by far the most dominant of the bunch. The SA5's dual cutaways evoked Gibson's popular ES-335 design, but the SA5 differed from many mid 1960s designs with its

A nod to Beatlemania: the SA15 and SA15D.

SA50

The SA50 features a different vibrato system than the 30.

two mini-humbuckers (which had separate volume knobs and a master tone), zero fret, and vibrato system. The trapezoidal fretboard inlays and standard f-holes reflected the trends of several American models from the 1950s and 1960s.

Within the next two years, Yamaha would introduce several more SA models, some of which varied wildly from the 335-esque SA5. The SA15 and 15D were single-cutaway archtops with elongated horns and slashing f-holes. The aesthetics were certainly influenced by the Rickenbacker guitars that the Beatles were pictured so prominently with at the time. The SA15 and 15D featured separate volume and tone knobs for each mini-humbucker, simple vibrato systems, and fretboard markers that were positioned at the bass side of the neck.

Another addition to Yamaha's mid 1960s family was the SA20: a 12-string version of the SA5. The SA30 and SA50 were other 6-string variations on this theme.

*More members of Yamaha's mid 1960s family:
the SA20 12-string and SA30.*

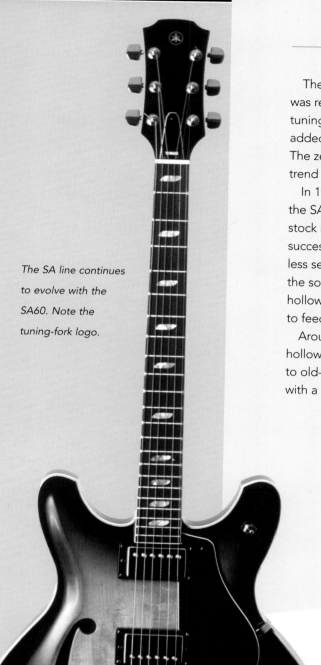

SA60

The SA line continues to evolve with the SA60. Note the tuning-fork logo.

The SA design would not undergo any real changes until the SA60 was released in 1973. This was the first guitar in the series to sport Yamaha's tuning-fork logo and full-sized humbucking pickups. The upscale SA90 added gold hardware and a wood-grain pickguard to the equation. The zero frets of previous models were gone, reflecting the worldwide trend of losing that feature.

In 1977, Yamaha would give the SA line a makeover with the introduction of the SA700. The horns of the two cutaways had been rounded off and the headstock had also been changed; the 700 now looked very much like the hugely successful American archtops. The construction of the SA guitars was more or less set and would remain relatively unchanged for many years. That included the solid block of wood running the length of the body (making the SA a semi-hollowbody). This block added stability and made the guitars less susceptible to feedback.

Around the time of the SA5's introduction in 1967, Yamaha unveiled its first hollowbody archtop electric guitar, the AE11. This model, intended to appeal to old-school jazz players, had a 17-inch lower bout and a narrower upper bout with a single sharp, Florentine cutaway.

The new and improved SA700 with rounded horns and a redesigned headstock.

The AE12 with
Venetian cutaway
and tuning-fork
logo.

The AE Models

The dual humbuckers, rosewood bridge, and trapeze tailpiece contributed to the resemblance between the AE11 and a 1960s-era Gibson Byrdland or ES-125. The AE11's headstock was the early Yamaha design that was also used on the first SA models, with the company name in block letters and no three-tuning-fork logo.

It was five years before Yamaha followed up with the AE12 and AE18 models. The most obvious design change in these early 1970s guitars was the rounded, Venetian cutaway on both models. The headstock had also evolved into a more sculpted shape with the only inlay being the three tuning forks. The AE12 and AE18 came with laminated spruce tops and birch and beech sides. The AE12 had a rosewood-on-maple neck whereas the AE18 sported an ebony-on-maple neck.

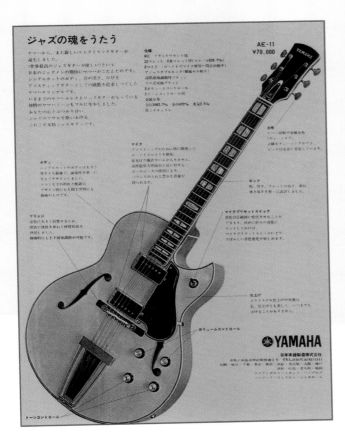

Yamaha's first jazz archtop, the AE11.

AE1200

The Big Time

None of Yamaha's archtop guitars up to this point were readily available in the U.S. The push into the American market would begin in the late 1970s, when the success of the solidbody SG2000 had opened doors with players and dealers. The AE1200 represented a step toward a real high-end archtop 6-string. With its rich sunburst finish, elegant trapeze tailpiece, and ornate headstock inlay, the AE1200 had the look and the vibe of the most sought-after jazz boxes on the market. The AE2000, which was introduced the same year, featured a solid spruce top and enhanced the perception that Yamaha was building serious instruments for professional players.

The SA line was also flirting with the high-end market at the end of the 1970s. The SA2000 turned heads with its gold hardware and rock-solid construction. In a market dominated by the American companies, however, it was still an uphill battle for Yamaha. Ken Dapron, Director of Yamaha Guitar Development, remembers the guitar climate—and Yamaha's strategy—at the time.

"We had set a standard in the late 1960s with our acoustic guitars of having an incredibly durable, good-sounding guitar at a low price," he says. "When

High-end jazz: the AE1200 archtop.

The SA2000, poised to make a splash in the U.S. market.

The solid-top AE2000.

our electrics entered the U.S. market in 1976, we started with the high-end, and the SA2000 is an example of that. To compete with Gibson, everything had to be better. We had better fretwork, totally clean binding, and the best finishes available on any production guitar in the world."

Yamaha's quality control team, which included direction from renowned luthier John Carruthers, saw to it that the SA2000s were set up flawlessly before they guitars got to the dealer. After an acclimation period of over a month, the frets were leveled and dressed, the instruments were restrung, and the finishes were buffed out. Only then were the guitars sent to stores, where they compared very favorably to the American models.

Thanks to the stellar workmanship of Yamaha's Japanese builders and the setup skills of the American team, the SA2000 became the first Yamaha semi-hollowbody guitar to truly appeal to top professional players. Robben Ford, Carlos Rios, and Tommy Tedesco all were seen onstage and in the studio with SA2000s. Phil Keaggy, another SA2000 user, featured the guitar prominently on his 1991 album *Play thru Me*.

Now that Yamaha had broken into the ranks of the top players with their semi-hollow and hollowbody guitars, the company stuck with the designs that had gotten them there. Variations on the SA and AE designs would appear for a few years, with most of the changes being cosmetic: chrome hardware instead of gold, black finishes as opposed to natural or sunburst, etc.

ABOVE:
*Robben Ford jams
on his SA1000.*

*Super sideman
Carlos Rios with
an SA2000.*

The Next Stage

When Yamaha opened the U.S. custom chop, the Yamaha Guitar Development (YGD), in 1990, it was an opportunity to extend the reach of the archtop guitar line. The designers at YGD began working on designs with Yamaha Japan that would eventually evolve into the AES1500.

The AES1500 would become a huge favorite for guitarists of a variety of styles. The hollowbody construction, not to mention the Bigsby vibrato on the AES1500B, made it a great choice for old-time rock-and-rollers and rockabilly players. The AES1500, however, featured unique electronics that enabled it to cover a tremendous amount of stylistic ground. The two DiMarzio DLX Plus pickups—alternately known as Q-100s—were a higher output, hum-canceling version of the venerable P-90 soapbar pickup. Push/push switches on the 1500's tone pots split the pickups' coils for a twangier, brighter sound.

The Q-100 pickups in the AES1500 at first seemed like a curious choice to DiMarzio's Steve Blucher. "The AES1500 was the first hollowbody instrument we used these pickups on," he explains. "I was nervous at first, because it's a fairly high-output pickup, and that can create feedback issues. But we tried them and everybody loved the sound."

One player who became a fan of the AES1500 is Nashville session cat Kenny Greenberg. A consummate pro who has worked with Hank Williams, Jr., Trisha Yearwood, Brooks and Dunn, Joan Baez, and many others, Greenberg has several AES1500s in his arsenal. "Mike Eldred gave me an AES1500 about fifteen years ago," says Greenberg, "and I immediately fell in love with it. To me, it's sort of like a cross between a 335, a Gretsch, and a Guild." Like all Nashville aces, Greenberg will have many guitars on hand for any given session, but the AES1500 finds its way onto a lot of records. "I wrote a song that became a hit for Amy Grant called 'House of Love.' It was a duet she did with Vince Gill, and I used my hardtail 1500 on that for both the rhythm and the solo. I had used it on the demo, and the producer wanted the album track to sound just like the demo. I played it through an old Vox AC30 amp, and it really worked. It's a song that gets a lot of airplay, and every time I hear it, I picture that white Yamaha guitar and I think, 'That sounds really good!'"

It's somewhat ironic that Greenberg's hardtail AES1500 gets so much airplay when it's his Bigsby-equipped AES1500Bs that see the most action. "My 1500 with the Bigsby is the one I record with the most," he says. "It doesn't sound exactly like a Gretsch, but it's like a cousin of a Gretsch—nice and bright and just a great recording tool. I've played that guitar on a bunch of records, like Jewel's *This Way*, Wynonna Judd's *Other Side*, and with the Indigo Girls. In fact, Emily [Saliers] from the Indigo Girls liked the sound of my Yamaha so much, she went out and got one after that session."

Nashville studio hotshot Kenny Greenberg with his AES1500.

These two prototypes from the mid-1990s led to the creation of the AES1500. Note the U-shape that the individual tailpiece's fingers form—that would become a left-to-right diagonal on solidbody AES models, and be replaced with a stop tailpiece on production model AES1500s.

Troy Van Leeuwen

From A Perfect Circle to Queens of the Stone Age: Troy Van Leeuwen with his AES1500.

Another gig for the perpetually busy Greg Leisz is his work with Bill Frisell on an album called *The Intercontinentals*. One of the guitarists on the project, Vinicius Cantuaria, is also a proponent of the AES1500. "Vinicius does great work on his 1500s," says Leisz. "That was his main instrument on the tour and the record. He does this lightly picked Brazilian thing, and the AES works great for that. But then he'll put all these effects on it and it sounds amazing for that, too. He'll use an octaver on it because we don't have a bassist. It really showed me how that guitar could go into other styles of music."

Speaking of other styles of music, rock players have also taken notice of the AES1500's powerful tone mojo. A Perfect Circle and Queens of the Stone Age guitarist Troy Van Leeuwen uses his 1500 onstage and in the studio to crank out his brand of neo-retro rock. Prior to playing his first AES1500, Van Leeuwen had been aware of Yamaha for some time. "As a kid," he says, "someone always had a Yamaha acoustic around. The first electric I tried was the AES1500, which I started playing when I joined A Perfect Circle. I had been playing Gibson ES-335s and Epiphones, and the more I played the Yamaha, the more I liked it. It really felt broken-in in the right way."

The extreme dynamic shifts that accompany APC's dramatic music required a sensitive but powerful guitar; and Van Leeuwen found his Yamahas to be more than up to the task. "There are a lot of dynamic jumps in A Perfect Circle," he says, "and I think hollowbodies in general are more diverse with dynamics. These guitars in particular are, because you can split the coils on them. I can go from soft fingerpicking stuff to a really heavy part easily. And feedback has never been a problem with this guitar. I mean, you want the feedback as long as you can control it, and the AES1500 deals with it really well. I've had to stuff foam in other guitars but never these. I don't know how to explain it, but these guitars just seem to have feedback control built into them."

For his work with Queens of the Stone Age, Van Leeuwen relies on his 1500s and an SA2200. "My Yamahas just work really well," he enthuses. "They're based on classic designs but with these unique twists, so they're tried-and-true but original at the same time. The 1500 especially has sounds I can't get from other instruments. You'd have to custom order it. We just finished a new Queens record, and we brought in every piece of gear that we own into the studio—vintage stuff, rare gear, everything. My AES1500 and SA2200 ended up being used a lot. They sounded great. They can stand up to anything."

When Orgy's Amir Derakh isn't cranking out low-tuned guitar-synth lines on his solidbody AES signature model, he's playing an AES1500. Derakh uses his hollowbody for playing and producing projects outside the Orgy world. "When I first saw the AES1500," he says, "I thought it was just a beautiful instrument. I want it to be part of my sound with Julien-K, which is my new project with Ryan [Shuck, Orgy co-guitarist]. I'm not playing guitar synth in this band, because that's my Orgy sound. I like for instruments to push me in other directions, and the AES1500 does that. It's an amazing, classic-looking guitar with a great sound."

The builders at Yamaha had also refined their double-cutaway semi-hollow SA2000. When the SA2200 was unveiled, it shared many of the design elements of the 2000, including the 24 3/4-inch scale length, laminated maple body, and dual humbuckers. The 2200 now features a highly figured maple top and push/push switches on the tone knobs to split the coils of the two alnico pickups. Bernie Chiaravalle—guitarist for Michael McDonald—and Robben Ford both picked up 2200s, with Chiaravalle calling it "a screamer for soloing." The player responsible for informing the most players of the SA2200, however, has got to be Lukasz Gottwald. As the guitarist of the "Saturday Night Live" band for nearly a decade, Gottwald delivers the guitar parts for all the music before and after commercial breaks, as well as for the show's skits and commercial jingles. When he's not doing the weekly TV show, Gottwald is writing, producing, and playing guitar on singles for Kelly Clarkson and the Backstreet Boys.

The SA2200 with highly figured maple top.

"I learned about the SA2200 from my guitar teacher, Rodney Jones," says Gottwald. "He's a jazz cat who owns a bunch ES-335s and other really expensive archtops. He told me, 'This Yamaha is my main axe. I love this thing.' That made a big impression on me. When I got the "SNL" gig, that's when I started playing Yamahas. I have a couple Pacificas for the Nile Rodgers-style funk stuff, but I mostly play the 2200. We do a lot of Booker T and the MGs and Philly soul, and the 2200 is perfect for that. It's a great blues guitar, and even when it's clean, it still sounds really meaty. It works great for pop stuff, too. In fact, for this Kelly Clarkson single there was a '59 Les Paul in the studio—believe it or not—and I used my Yamaha for at least 75 percent of the guitar tracks on that song!"

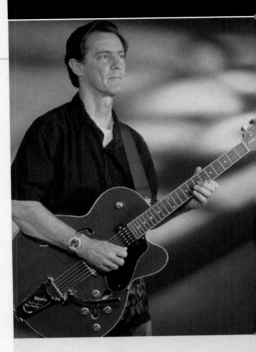

Sideman Greg Leisz with an AES1500.

Lukasz Gottwald from the "Saturday Night Live" band with his SA2000.

True Jazz

The piezo pickup mounted under the AEX1500's bridge saddle provides acoustic guitar tones. The AEX1500's mini-humbucker is attached to the neck, so as not to interfere with the vibration of the top.

Although both the SA and the AES archtops are perfectly suited for jazz playing, they found greater popularity among rock and blues guitarists, who were drawn to their hot looks and versatile tones. The instrument that truly grabbed jazz players was Yamaha's AEX1500, a revamped, updated addition to the jazz-approved AE line of archtops.

The AEX1500, designed in Japan by Kiyoshi Minakuchi, is a great example of Yamaha's ability to meld vintage and modern elements. From a visual standpoint, the AEX1500 looks like a classic jazz box with its elegant lines and dignified, uncluttered appearance. The ebony fretboard and bridge set off the gold hardware nicely. The single mini-humbucker is attached to the neck—not the maple top—allowing the top to vibrate more naturally.

Where the AEX1500 differs from a traditional jazz 6-string is in its electronics. In addition to the neck mini-humbucker, the AEX1500 features a piezo pickup located under the bridge saddle to deliver amplified acoustic guitar tones. An onboard, three-band EQ provides precise fine-tuning of the piezo sound, and a mix knob allows the player to blend the magnetic pickup with the piezo for an unprecedented array of tones.

It seems only natural that such a unique, world-class jazz instrument would attract a player befitting its stature. The champion of the AEX1500 arrived in the form of Scottish jazz master Martin Taylor. Taylor, one of the greatest fingerstyle jazz players of all time, provided input on the design of the

Fingerstyle master Martin Taylor with the AEX1500.

AEX1500 for Yamaha. (In fact, the guitar is called the "Yamaha Martin Taylor model" in the U.K.)

"I'm very proud of it [the AEX1500]. It came out well," Taylor told *Vintage Guitar* magazine in September 1996. "I've been a Yamaha endorsee for six or seven years. I have two AEX1500 production models: one blond and one sunburst. I also have two prototypes. I only travel with my Yamahas. They're easy to play and they sound consistently good, no matter where I'm playing. I know that sounds like an ad, but it's true. That's why I play them."

When in the studio, Taylor has a huge collection of instruments at his disposal—many of his own, as well as the world-famous Scott Chinery collection, which he played on *Masterpiece Guitars*. Even so, he still manages to finds track space for his Yamahas. He detailed one such session, which happened to be a duet with his hero Chet Atkins, in an interview with *The Guitar Magazine* in April of 1996. "While we were in the studio, I brought out my Yamaha AEX1500. We put two mics on the guitar and put it through a rack of EQs and compressors, and also used a room mic. It was such a beautiful sound that I thought I might as well sit there and record some more. I played the results to my record company and told them I might have an album. They loved it." The results of that session appeared on Taylor's album *Portraits*—a great showcase of his unbelievable chops and the pure tone of the AEX1500. Other fans of the AEX1500 include George Pajon, Jr., of the Black Eyed Peas and Michael O'Neil from George Benson's band.

The AEX family doesn't end with the 1500. The bolt-on-neck AEX500 is an understated, less ornate model that keeps the neck mini-humbucker and piezo bridge electronics, but with a more down-home look thanks to its brown sunburst finish and straight-ahead tailpiece. The 500 uses alder for the body wood with a spruce top.

Rounding out the AEX line are the more rock-ready 520 and 502 models. Both guitars have Tune-o-Matic-style bridges with stop tailpieces, alder bodies, and maple tops. The 520 comes with two mini-humbuckers, and the 502 uses two soapbar single-coils.

The AEX1500 archtop.

AEX500 *AEX502* *AEX520*

"I have some really good friends in the bass world who all make great instruments, but after these Yamaha basses had been on so many hit records and successful tours, it's easy to get a little superstitious about it and not want to use anything else."

– Nathan East

Bass Guitars

The History of Yamaha Guitars

SA2

Yamaha's first bass, the SA2.

The Lowdown

In the 1960s, the electric bass was still decidedly in its infancy. Fender had released the first production model electric bass only a decade prior, and the instrument had not seen the rush of popularity that the electric guitar had enjoyed. Partly due to its supportive, less-flashy role, the bass continued to thump along in the background while singers, songwriters, and frontmen flocked to the guitar. The Beatles juggernaut changed all that, thanks to charismatic singer/bassist Paul McCartney. McCartney was the first star to truly bring the bass to center stage as he played his inventive lines while singing the songs that would become the soundtrack of a generation. Suddenly, the bass was no longer in the background. It was inextricably linked to memorable hooks and rock-and-roll stardom.

This was the climate into which Yamaha dropped the SB2: the company's first electric bass design, which debuted in 1966. The SB2 was a double-cutaway instrument with two single-coil pickups. Its short-scale, 31 1/2-inch neck had twenty frets and was topped with a pointed headstock.

Yamaha introduced the SB2A (along with its upscale siblings, the SB5A and SB7A) the following year. Whereas the SB2 was vaguely reminiscent of the Fender Jazz Bass, the SB2A made no attempt to hop on the Fender bandwagon. Instead, it sported the same body and headstock stylings as the wild and funky SG2A and SG5 guitars. Yamaha would follow with the strangely beautiful SB1C in 1968.

SB1C

SB7A

SA70

Today, these early Yamaha basses are still sought after and collected by fans of offbeat body styles and 1960s-era kitsch.

Several instrument manufacturers were making hollowbody basses in the 1960s including Hofner, Guild, Gibson, and Vox. Any "Ed Sullivan" (or, for that matter "American Bandstand" or "Top of the Pops") episode might show a hollowbody 4-string in the hands of McCartney, the Rolling Stones' Bill Wyman (who, interestingly, would later play a Yamaha BB3000), or Paul Samwell-Smith of the Yardbirds. Although these instruments posed problems due to feedback and durability issues, many players were drawn to their relatively light weight and warm tones. Yamaha released its own hollowbody bass, the SA70, in 1967.

The double-cutaway SA70 came with two humbucking pickups, master volume and tone controls, and a pickup balance knob for a surprising array of tonal options. These semi-acoustic basses were not big hits with players and, by 1972, had been discontinued.

By 1972, Yamaha had expanded its bass line to include the single-cutaway SB30. These were the first Yamaha basses to feature two-to-a-side tuning machines and humbucking pickups. The SB30's rounded, flowing curves had more in common with Yamaha's acoustic guitars than with any of the company's previous bass designs.

The mid 1970s brought back the double-cutaway bass with several SB models, such as the SB55, 75, 500, 600, 800, and 1200S. These designs, with their offset body curves and four-to-a-side tuning machines, foreshadowed the model that would finally make Yamaha a major player in the bass market.

The shape of things to come: the SB1200S bass provided an inkling of the BB series that would follow.

SB30

SB55

The BB Era

Rock show:
Paul McCartney
onstage with
his BB1200.

Just as Yamaha had unveiled the right guitar at the right time with the SG2000, the company pulled a similar coup in the bass world with the release of the "Broad Bass," or BB1200, in 1977. The bass market was still dominated by the American manufacturers, but more and more players were losing the sense that Fender and Gibson could do no wrong. And, despite the almost-universal presence of bolt-on-neck basses onstage and in recording studios, bassists were definitely starting to take notice of the sonic and ergonomic benefits of the neck-through design like the one on the BB1200. (Fender's infamous 1970s-era, three-bolt necks no doubt sped up that change.) The BB1200 (like the BB1000) instantly knocked bassists out with its feel, sound, and attention to detail. There was no such thing as a high-end production bass at the time, and players who felt let down by American manufacturers were overjoyed with the BB1200's quality, sustain, and jaw-dropping setup.

It worked. The BB basses were a hit with bass players who loved the resonant, sustaining tone. Paul McCartney himself would play a BB1200S in the early 1980s, as seen in the video for his tune "Coming Up."

No Doubt's Tony Kanal remembers the BB1600 as being his first bass—and it would be his main bass for years. "Gwen's [Stefani, singer] dad was working for Yamaha at the time in the motor division, and he was able to get me a deal. I chose the BB1600. It served me loyally for ten years until I found the BB3000. I fell in love with it when we were touring Japan in 1996. I still have my original BB1600, and I'm now in the process of having another one made in its likeness by the Yamaha custom shop—YGD. I was told that my original was crafted from an exquisite piece of wood seldom found in production basses. I always thought it was a really special bass. I got lucky on that one."

The Yamaha BB1000.

The first high-end production bass: the BB1200.

Abraham Laboriel

Laboriel with a TRB5 five-string.

Session superhero Abraham Laboriel might just be the most recorded bassist in history. By his own estimate, he has logged over 4,000 sessions in a career that spans several decades. Far too numerous to list, these recording gigs include legendary albums by Henery Mancini, vibraphonist Gary Burton, Ella Fitzgerald, and Aretha Franklin, not to mention tons of pop and R&B records. Yamaha basses have played a huge part in his amazing body of work. "My relationship with Yamaha started in 1977," says Laboriel. "The R&D team from Japan came to L.A. and asked players like Leland Sklar and me to evaluate some instruments.

We played the basses and made comments, and the technicians wrote it all down faithfully. I thought that was a great thing. I suggested they improve the bridge to enhance sustain, lower the action so it could be played with a lighter attack, and change the tuning machines. Lee Sklar suggested they reverse the split pickup so the bass coil was lower and the treble side was higher—the opposite of how it is on a Fender Precision—for a richer sound. When Yamaha showed up with the new basses, they had incorporated all of our

suggestions. That completely blew our minds. Most manufacturers weren't willing to do that."

When Laboriel was touring Japan with Lee Ritenour, he got his hands on a production model BB2000. After the tour he brought the bass home, and it became one of his most important recording tools.

"I played that BB2000 on Lionel Ritchie's 'All Night Long,' and a lot of the Al Jarreau albums at the time," he says. "Between 1978 and 1995, most of the producers I worked with would tell me to bring that bass. I would generally show up at a three-hour session with three basses—a Fender Precision and two Yamahas. I would bring my BB2000 and a BB2000 that Valley Arts converted into a five-string. When I did projects that would last ten days, I would bring 12 basses, and half of them would be Yamahas. The people at Yamaha had made a really serious commitment to building great instruments for professional players, so the sound quality on all those recordings was impeccable. It has been a very fruitful relationship with Yamaha because of their willingness to listen to what players want."

The listening paid off. When the BB2000 came out in 1980, it was all that was needed to catapult Yamaha into the upper echelons of bass builders. More and more pro players were flocking to the BB2000 (and, two years later, to the BB3000), struck by its quality, tone, and playability. The 2000 and 3000 came in the now-standard P-J pickup configuration of one split humbucker (the "P," or Precision pickup) and one single-coil (the "J," or Jazz).

Van Halen bassist Michael Anthony was taken with the BB2000 during an early VH tour. "We were in Japan when I first tried it," he says. "I loved the way it felt. I also appreciated the fact that it had two pickups—I liked the tonal options that gave me. I had been playing Charvel basses, but the Yamaha became my main bass. I did a lot of recording with it—it's all over our *1984* album. Everyone was pleased with my bass sound, and I think it sounds really good on 'Panama' and on 'Girl Gone Bad,' especially in the jam section."

Van Halen's Michael Anthony in the mid 1980s with his BB2000.

The Yamaha BB3000 bass.

Nathan East

Anthony wasn't the only high-profile bassist to be impressed with the 2000. Nathan East, member of Four Play and veteran sideman to Eric Clapton (as well as Phil Collins, George Harrison, Elton John, Steve Winwood, Joe Pass, Michael Jackson, Whitney Houston, Babyface, Quincy Jones, Al Jarreau, Stevie Wonder, Justin Timberlake, Barbra Streisand, Sheryl Crow, Bob Dylan, Ray Charles, Barry White, George Benson, Frank Sinatra, Sammy Davis Jr., Tom Jones, Dolly Parton, Kenny Rogers, Usher, Kenny Loggins, James Taylor, Randy Newman, Lionel Ritchie, Lou Reed, B.B. King, Bonnie Raitt, and Madonna, to name just a few) is another fan. "The first Yamaha bass I ever played was a BB2000," says East. "It was Abraham Laboriel's, and I tried to take it from him [*laughs*]! I loved the sound and the feel—everything about it was exactly what I wanted."

Laboriel hooked East up with Yamaha's Takashi "Hagi" Hagiwara on a subsequent tour of Japan. Hagiwara presented East with a sunburst BB3000 for his gig that night in Tokyo with Lee Ritenour. "I walked right onstage with that bass," recalls East. "I played it straight out of the box, with no tweaks, no setup—nothing. I informed Hagi that it was going home with me! That bass was perfect."

Yamaha would release other BB-series basses throughout the 1980s. Although they wouldn't get the same attention from pro players as the 2000 and 3000, less-expensive versions, such as the BB300 and 450 were very popular. Justin Meldal-Johnsen, bassist with Beck and Tori Amos, remembers his BB300 fondly. "My parents got me a BB300 for my birthday in the mid 1980s," he says. "It just blew away everything in its price range—unparalleled quality. It was easy to play and really resonant." Although he regrets selling that first Yamaha bass, Meldal-Johnsen has

The bass that launched a thousand hits: Nathan East and the BB3000.

since added other models to his growing collection, including a BB5000 five-string, and a couple of BB3000s. "I was touring in Japan eight or nine years ago, and there's a Yamaha store in the Shibuya area of Tokyo. They had these BB3000s that had been discontinued in the U.S., but they were still available in Japan. I got in touch with Ken Dapron and he ordered me two of them—one in black sparkle and one in a dark cherry sunburst. They're a big part of what I use in the studio, and I brought them on the road for Beck's *Midnite Vultures* tour, too. They were the basses that never needed any setup throughout the tour. They're just amazing basses. I tend to prefer quirky instruments, and a lot of modern basses bum me out. But these are modern without being glassy. They have a lot of personality."

Touring pros like East and Meldal-Johnsen, who regularly played in Japan, had access to a greater range of Yamaha basses than Stateside players. In the 1980s, Yamaha began beefing up their artist relations program in the U.S. to better serve the needs of musicians. Doug Buttleman was running the AR department for Yamaha in 1984, and he reached out to an up-and-coming bassist named Billy Sheehan, who was beginning to gain some recognition for his dazzling chops and relentless gigging. "I was familiar with Yamaha basses," says Sheehan. "I played my old P-Bass pretty much exclusively, but I was in a music store one day, and I tried a BB3000. I couldn't believe how well it played. I had just tried an Alembic, which was like the Rolls-Royce of basses at the time. This Yamaha compared very favorably to the Alembic. It was really alive and the quality was just amazing. Even though I didn't buy it, that bass was in the back of my mind when Doug contacted me in 1984." Buttleman impressed upon Sheehan that Yamaha wanted to work with him, with the full knowledge that Sheehan was very loyal to his tried-and-true Fender. "I call my P-Bass my wife," says Sheehan, "and she did not like me playing this Yamaha at all [*laughs*]! It was like she said to me, 'After all I've done for you, and now you've got this hot, young chick hanging around!' But Doug was really cool about things. He didn't care if I still played my Fender. There were no stipulations or restrictions. For such a huge corporation, it really felt like the kind of deal you would do with one of your buddies."

The first thing Yamaha made for Sheehan was a modified BB3000. Taking measurements from his Fender, Yamaha added girth to the BB's neck profile, and outfitted the bass with extra pickups, stereo outs, and a Hipshot Bass Extender Key. "I was on the cover of *Guitar Player* magazine with that pink BB," says Sheehan. "It played great. I gigged and recorded with that bass in the David Lee Roth days. I loved it, but the body was a little wider than I was used to, so it hit my legs and ribs in the wrong spots. Ultimately, we went back to the drawing board." When Sheehan and Yamaha got back to the drawing board, many of the features on his custom BB3000 would already be there.

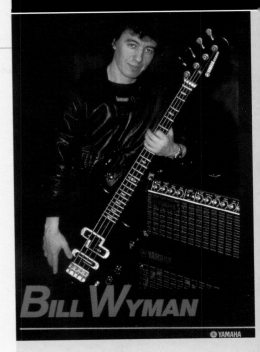

Bill Wyman of the
Rolling Stones with
a Yamaha BB3000.

Readers' choice: Sheehan
and Yamaha on the cover
of Guitar Player magazine,
December, 1986.

RBX800A

RBX

As the decade of the 1980s continued, bassists, like guitarists, were drawn to wilder shapes and more radical curves on their instruments. When Yamaha introduced the RBX line in 1987, it was a perfect fit for 1980s rockers—lean, mean, and fast.

The RBX series has always included several models with varying features. All but the RBX170 (which has an agathis body) come with an alder body and a rosewood-on-maple, 24-fret, bolt-on neck. From there, players can choose between active and passive electronics, various pickup configurations, and color options. Fretless and five-string models were also available. The easy playability, rock-and-roll good looks, and entry-level pricing have made the RBX one of Yamaha's most successful bass lines.

YGD

When Yamaha opened the U.S. custom shop—Yamaha Guitar Development—in 1990, the wheels were already in motion to partner with big-name musicians on signature instruments. Yamaha's relationship with Sheehan was in full swing; he was one of the most high-profile bassists on the planet, with his face—and bass—gracing the covers of every music magazine imaginable.

Yamaha and Sheehan had sown the seeds of his ultimate bass with the BB3000 experiment. Now it was time to create an instrument they could all be completely happy with. YGD was prepared to do whatever it took to not only get Sheehan what he wanted, but also to send a message to the bass-playing world that there was a new standard in bass craft.

The RBX300

"When Yamaha opened the custom shop," recalls Sheehan, "we decided to use my P-Bass as a template and include all the improvements I had made on it over the years, but remove all the things that were still weak points." One thing Sheehan wanted changed was the neck-to-body joint. Because of his unorthodox neck-bending techniques, that was a constant concern regarding his basses. "Bending the neck isn't exactly recommended, so it's not a fair criticism of an instrument," he admits. "But I wanted it improved just the same." Done. YGD devised a novel way to attach a bolt-on neck that afforded unprecedented strength and rigidity without hampering upper-fret access.

To ensure that the new bass wouldn't go out of Sheehan's comfort zone, Yamaha took specs from his Fender and incorporated them into the design. "I brought in my pickguard," says Sheehan, "and we duplicated it so wherever my hand fell on the Fender, it would feel the same on the new bass. We placed the knobs the exact same distance from the pickups, so it all felt really natural."

In his mad scientist way, Sheehan had scalloped part of the fretboard on his Fender, and that was also done on the prototype, with the wood from the 17th through 21st frets scooped out to facilitate string bending and vibrato.

Monster bends made easy: the scalloped fretboard of the Attitude Bass.

The Attitude Bass

YGD nailed Sheehan's stereo pickup configuration with a custom DiMarzio woofer in the neck and a P-Bass-style pickup in the middle, with separate outputs for each. DiMarzio's Steve Blucher explains how those "WillPower" pickups came to be: "Bill had been using our Model 1 pickup in the neck position for a while," he says. "That's a direct replacement for the Gibson EB-0 pickup. When we designed the neck pickup for the Attitude bass, we made it a little cleaner and more articulate. We also widened it a little to reflect the string spacing. For the other pickup, which is in the middle position, we based the design on our Model P, but this time we voiced it a little darker and chunkier sounding."

With the addition of the Hipshot Bass Extender Key, the instrument appeared ready for action. But, even with all the care and refinements, would Sheehan, a self-described creature of habit and perpetual tweaker, be able to walk onstage with a bass other than his "wife"?

"I had to leave for a Mr. Big tour in Japan before it was finished," says Sheehan. "The deal was that the Japanese facility would have the bass ready for me when I got there. It was supposed to be so perfect that I could walk right onstage with it. I normally tweak a bass for at least a week before I'll even think about gigging with it. I was more nervous for that show than

ATT DLX MR

for any show I've ever done."

Nervous, as it turned out, for no reason. The bass was set up perfectly and the gig went off without a hitch. Yamaha had done the impossible—they got Sheehan to cheat on his "wife." "That bass played unbelievably well," he says. "It was rock solid. I played it every night on that tour. I recorded a number-one single, 'To Be with You,' on it. I recorded the really blazing stuff on the *Lean into It* album on my Yamaha. It works great for fast, intricate stuff like that because it really speaks. You can hear every note, and that's something common to all these Yamaha basses. A lot of basses can't do that."

Thus the Attitude bass was born. Yamaha would turn this YGD creation into several production models, including the Attitude Limited, Custom, Deluxe, and Standard. Both four- and five-string models were available.

And, whatever model bassists chose, they could be secure in the knowledge that they were playing the same bass as the man whose name was on it. "All my instruments are production models," says Sheehan. "That's something I insisted on. It had to be something that any kid could walk into any store and get. I learned that the hard way from working with some other manufacturers. The ones played by anyone famous were custom made and were really good. The ones sold in the store were made by some guy doing sloppy work with a hand drill. I always thought that was really unfair, and Yamaha absolutely does not do that."

ATT Standard

East Meets West

Nathan East was already a devoted Yamaha player when YGD opened in 1990, having played his BB series basses on countless records and tours. "I had been playing my BB3000s for two or three years before we started talking about a custom bass," says East. "I worked with Hagi, Ken Dapron, Leo Knapp, and Tsugitomo Gotoh from Japan. I wanted to add a string to increase the range. We talked about the string spacing and the electronics. I wanted a P-J pickup configuration. When we got all these elements working together, it became the BB5000 five-string."

The birth of the BB5000 was an exciting time for Yamaha and East both. East, who was working with Kenny Loggins at the time, had just made a pair of connections that would bring him even greater success. The first was with Phil Collins and Phillip Bailey who, along with East, would soon pen the number-one single "Easy Lover," on which East would play his new BB5000. The second connection was with arguably the most famous guitarist in the world, Eric Clapton.

With East's stock continually on the rise, it was only natural to create a signature model for him. After many discussions, the BB East was created. The 5-string, neck-through bass features an alder and maple body with a mahogany and maple neck and ebony fingerboard. The BB East's active electronics were a departure from the BB5000's passive system. East would also obtain a fretless version of his signature model.

East continued to tour and record with his Yamahas and the hits just kept coming. He cites his work with Anita Baker and Clapton as good examples of his ultimate bass tone. World-class producers like Quincy Jones have nothing but praise for the sound of East's Yamahas. "I have

Yamaha's first 5-string, the BB5000.

Nathan East's first signature model bass, the BB NE.

The hits keep coming: the latest Nathan East model, the BB NEII 6-string.

some really good friends in the bass world who all make great instruments," says East. "But after these Yamaha basses had been on so many hit records and successful tours, it's easy to get a little superstitious about it and not want to use anything else. What people like Quincy have told me is that my bass tone complements the other instruments really well. It's punchy but fat, and you can really hear every note. It's never overbearing—it occupies just the right amount of space in the track."

East's signature model has evolved into the current BB NEII 5- and 6-string basses, which he brought on the road for the most recent Clapton tour. "We played the Royal Albert Hall in London and Sting jammed with us. He checked out my bass and really liked it. I gave him one and he was very appreciative. I'm having a left-handed version made to present to Paul McCartney. That would be an all-time thrill if he would play one of my signature basses."

Year after year, East lays down the kind of bass lines that make him the first-call guy for some of the best musicians in the world. And his Yamaha instruments make it easy for him to feel comfortable doing his thing, no matter who is onstage with him. "I just try to play up to the standard I've set for myself from day one. That doesn't change, even if I'm playing with Clapton, or George Harrison, or George Benson. I do my best whether it's George Benson or Fred Benson. You've got to come with it, no matter what the gig."

Other BB series basses during this time include the BB2004 and BB2005. These basses shared many features of the BBNEII—neck-through construction, maple-capped alder bodies, active electronics, maple necks with mahogany strips, and the elegant-looking individual bridge saddles.

Yamaha offered even more affordable versions with the BB604/605 and the BB404/405. The bolt-on necks and passive electronics of these models contributed to their lower price points and appealed to fans of old-school features with modern workmanship.

Bolt-on beauty: the entry-level BB605.

The BB family of basses grows to include the BB2004 and BB2005.

The BEX

Yamaha refused to get stuck in their ways of making basses, despite the fact that those ways had become very successful. When longtime endorsee Billy Sheehan stopped by YGD to say hello one day, the conversation turned to a favorite subject—crazy, cool bass ideas.

"I've always been a huge Yardbirds fan," explains Sheehan. "Their bassist, Paul Samwell-Smith, played a hollowbody Epiphone Rivoli.

"The guys at YGD actually gave me an old Rivoli as a birthday gift—very cool! I thought it would be great to take that idea and do it in a more modern way. Yamaha had come up with this idea of hollowing out a bass body and laying an acoustic top over it. It gives you a lot of the sonic properties of an acoustic instrument but was easier and less expensive to do. So, the bass has a slab running down the middle and it's hollow on the sides, similar to an ES-335. That's what became the BEX-BS. It's a really unique instrument and I just love it. It's amazing to me that this huge corporation would not only be willing to build this bass, but to put it out as a production model."

Billy Sheehan cradles a BEX-BS semi-hollowbody bass.

RBXJM2

The John Myung signature model: the RBX JM2.

Progressive Connection

With the role of the bass expanding in all forms of music, more and more bassists were seeking out extended range 5- and 6-string instruments. Yamaha had had 6-string models in its line, including the bolt-on-neck TRB1006 and the through-neck TRB6PII. Many world-class bassists became fans of the TRB 5- and 6-string basses, such as jazz master Jimmy Haslip and studio veterans Will Lee and Abraham Laboriel. And it was a TRB 6-string that first brought Dream Theater bassist John Myung into the Yamaha fold.

Being in charge of holding down the bottom end in Dream Theater's elaborate arrangements, as well as needing to play intricate unison, harmony, and counterpoint lines, Myung needed an instrument that not only had great tone, but also incredible range and effortless playability. A 6-string user already, Myung spied a TRB 6-string in a music store and gave it a try. "I thought it was really well made," he says. "I had been playing some high-end 6-strings, but none of them was quite right. I had always just risen to the occasion and gotten used to playing whatever instrument I had."

Myung developed a relationship with the artist relations department at YGD, and they set him up with some basses to try. When the opportunity arose to design a signature instrument, he jumped at the

Home on the extended range: the TRB1006.

chance. "Not many people have the opportunity to work with a company like Yamaha, and it was a great learning experience for me. Tapping into the generations of wisdom there taught me a lot about the instrument."

Myung and YGD discussed the features that would make up his signature bass: the RBX JM (and later, the RBX JM2). After agreeing on an alder body with a rosewood-on-maple bolt-on neck, the next aspect they addressed was the string spacing. "We wanted the neck to feel comfortable, so we narrowed the string spacing a little," says Myung.

The next order of business was the electronics. Myung and Yamaha settled on a single Seymour Duncan SMB-6A humbucker. The pickup, when coupled with the active three-band, onboard EQ, gave Myung the tone he needed. "This system deals with a hard attack really well," he says. "I play percussively, and it makes that style of playing sound musical. It really tracks what I'm trying to do."

The technical demands of Dream Theater's music require a unique bass, not to mention a unique bassist. Myung feels like he's found his sound with the RBX JM2. "What I like about this bass is that it sits in the mix with drums, guitars, and keys. There's a lot going on in our music, but this bass tracks so well that you can still identify it."

John Myung with his RBX JM2.

BB3000MA

Michael Anthony

With Yamaha basses in the hands of so many top players, word of the goings on at YGD would naturally spread through the bass community whenever something was happening. So when Yamaha was talking about reissuing the bass that had put them on the map—the venerable BB3000—fans of that classic bass were excited, to say the least. And there was no bigger fan of BB basses than Van Halen bassist Michael Anthony.

"Right after we had finished the tour in 1998," says Anthony, "my friend Scott Uchida came to me and said that Yamaha was going to be making BB3000s again. I definitely wanted to get one, because my two original BBs were pretty banged up. Scott told me that Yamaha was interested in making a signature model for me, and I was totally into that."

Anthony wanted a few changes to the design and began meeting with YGD. Together, they went over the structural and tonal aspects of the instrument. "I wanted the neck to be somewhere between a Fender Precision and a Fender Jazz," says Anthony, "so we slimmed it down a bit but kept it nice and round. We also made the cutaway by the bottom horn deeper because I like to be able to reach all the frets." A Hipshot Bass Extender Key was added to facilitate drop-tuned VH songs such as "Unchained."

Anthony went back and forth with YGD's Erik Goehrisch on the winding of

Van Halen's Michael Anthony with his signature bass, the BB3000MA.

the pickups. Being a big believer in getting a sound that works in the context of a band, Anthony was in a bit of a quandary—Van Halen was not playing. Singer Gary Cherone had left the band and Eddie Van Halen was dealing with his much-publicized health problems, leaving Anthony with no gigs to try his new bass. "I thought the pickups Erik wound sounded great playing by myself," he recalls. "But you never really know about a tone until you try it on a gig. My first chance to hear the bass in a band situation was on a Sammy Hagar gig that I guested on. It sounded amazing. Sammy put out a live album and DVD from that show, and you can hear how great this bass sounds."

The bass that would become the BB3000MA wasn't complete until they agreed on the cosmetics. On the ebony fretboard, YGD inlaid red chili peppers, including a bunch of three at the twelfth fret that was copied directly from a tattoo on Anthony's shoulder. "When I saw that," says Anthony, "it really felt like my signature bass."

Yamaha also introduced a bolt-on, rosewood-on-maple-neck version of the Anthony bass, the BB1000MA, in the summer of 2001.

Anthony remains proud to have his name associated with Yamaha. "I really like working with the people at YGD. And this is just one of the best sounding and feeling basses I've ever owned. I turned Robby Takac from the Goo Goo Dolls onto it. He ended up using the bolt-on version and he really likes it. When we're on the road and guys in the opening bands ask me about my bass, I always tell them they can try it onstage. I like being a spokesman for it. Kind of like a goodwill ambassador!"

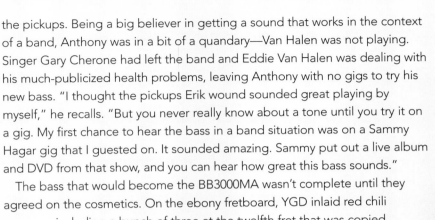

Goo Goo Dolls' Robby Takac and his BB1000MA bass.

Extending the Range

Other well-known Yamaha endorsees include John Patitucci, the insanely talented 6-string bass wizard from Chick Corea's Elektric Band. A longtime Yamaha player, Patitucci now plays his intricate runs and mind-boggling solos on his signature 6-string, the TRB JP2. Arriving at the bass that would become the JP2 entailed an interesting journey for Patitucci.

"It was the first time I was allowed to get in on the design of an instrument," says Patitucci. "I got hooked up with Yamaha through Dave Weckl, the drummer in Chick's band. He already played their drums, and Yamaha Japan thought it would be good if Chick's entire rhythm section was playing Yamaha stuff. So, Hagi in Japan told Mr. Naito—who was doing artist relations—to sign me. A little while later, we started working on a signature design."

Both Patitucci and Yamaha were fans of classic basses, and they worked to maintain that classic vibe as they created a modern 6-string. "We wanted to go with ash and alder for the body wood," explains Patitucci. "That would provide the solid fundamental like on those old Fender basses. Then we thought it would be cool to have a layer of maple to open up the high end. We came up with what we called a 'sandwich' of those three woods. After the woods, the electronics were a big part of the design. We worked with Mr. Gotoh in Japan on the preamp—he's really amazing.

Bass master John Patitucci solos on a TRB6PII.

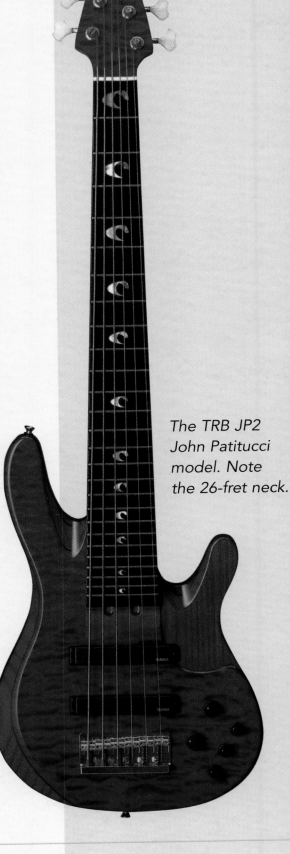

The preamp had bass, treble, and three different midrange settings—one normal, one with the mids notched for slapping, and one solo setting. My first signature bass was built by Leo Knapp, who is just a fantastic builder."

Thus the TRB JP was born. Patitucci would play the 6-string exclusively for eight years. Then Yamaha wanted to create an updated version of the JP. "When Ken told me he wanted to try to improve it, I wasn't sure where to go," recalls Patitucci. "That bass was tough to beat. We decided to extend the scale length from 34 inches to 35 inches to add a little punch to the low B. We added two frets to the neck, so now it has 26 frets. Then we addressed the preamp. Ken and Gotoh came out to my place in New York, and we sat in my basement for hours figuring out where the notch points should be and where we should roll off frequencies. It was really exciting. We ended up with a three-band EQ with a sweepable midrange that was very flexible."

The last change to the design was arguably the biggest one. The original Patitucci model was a neck-through construction. Now the idea was to go with a bolt-on. "There's just this fundamental tone to the old Jazz Basses that you only get with a bolt-on," says Patitucci. "Yamaha came up with a great six-bolt system that provides a much tighter seal. It was a big improvement in the sound—very tight and focused. This bass is on my latest solo album, *Songs, Stories, and Spirituals*, and I'm really happy with the tone. What we tried to do with this bass is to incorporate things that aren't just important to me, but that could work for everybody."

Between the RBX170—the most affordable bass in the line—and the TRB JP2, Yamaha has something for everyone whose job it is to hold down the bottom end. And the commitment to quality, tone, and service has inspired uncommon loyalty in the bass world. "When I get involved with something," says Sheehan, "I like to stick with it. But the bottom line here is that these basses just play and sound great. Piano players will often test a piano with their left hand, because it's so hard to make those low frequencies speak. The high notes just come through more easily. Maybe it's because Yamaha is also a piano company that their basses really reflect that. It's just in their makeup."

The TRB JP2 John Patitucci model. Note the 26-fret neck.

Serial Number Chart
for Acoustic and Classical Guitars

In the following charts, you can determine the year of manufacture for a Yamaha acoustic or classical guitar.

The first step is to find the serial number—a combination of letters and/or numbers—and the "Made in..." label (Japan, Taiwan, or Indonesia) on the guitar. You should be able to find these near the soundhole label or the stamp inside the guitar.

Once you have those two pieces of information, find the country of origin and serial number in one of the following charts and, using the Letter-to-Number Reference Chart below, calculate the year of manufacture for your guitar.

LETTER-TO-NUMBER Reference Chart

Often, some of the letters in the serial numbers represent specific numbers which, in turn, stand for the month and year of manufacture. See the chart below for the code.

H	I	J	K	L	M	N	O	P	Q	X	Y	Z
1	2	3	4	5	6	7	8	9	0	10	11	12

SAMPLE

Serial Number: IM705J   1991, July

I	M	7	0	5	J

└ Internal Production Code

└ This three-digit number represents the unit number

└ Month, June (M=6)

└ Year 1992 (I=2)

1941–1965   No documentation available

System # A1
1966–1985
Custom Shop
Made in Japan

Sequential Serial Numbers
#001–1042

System # A2

1986–1990

Custom Shop

Made in Japan

Serial Number: I6001   1986, February

```
I  6  0  0  1
```
| Unit Number

Year, 1986

Month, February (I=2)

System # A3

1991–1996

Custom Shop

Made in Japan

Serial Number: HN701J   1991, July

Note: Each month started with 700.

```
H  N  7  0  1  J
```
| Internal Code

Unit Number

Month, July (N=7)

Year 1991 (H=1)

System # A4

1997–2003

Custom Shop

Made in Japan

Serial Number: NH001   1997, January

```
N  H  0  0  1
```
| Unit Number

Month, January (H=1)

Year, 1997 (N=7)

System # A5

2004–

Custom Shop

Made in Japan

Serial Number: QKX001C   2004, October

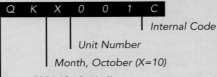

Internal Code

Unit Number

Month, October (X=10)

Year, 2004 (Q=0, K=4)

System # A6

1946–1968

Tenryu/Wada Factory

Made in Japan

This is a five digit sequential system.

There is no specific year of manufacturing data available.

System # A7

1969–1984

Tenryu/Wada Factory

Made in Japan

Serial Number: 690301   1969, March

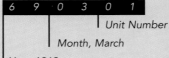

Unit Number

Month, March

Year, 1969

System # A8

1985–1986

Tenryu/Wada Factory

Made in Japan

Serial Number: 850001   1985

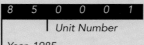

Unit Number

Year, 1985

System # A9

1971–2001
Kaohsiung Factory
Made in Taiwan

Serial Number: 11001001   1971, October 01

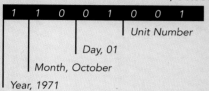

| 1 | 1 | 0 | 0 | 1 | 0 | 0 | 1 |

- Unit Number
- Day, 01
- Month, October
- Year, 1971

Note: This system allows for duplicate numbers.

System # A10

2001–
Kaohsiung Factory
Made in Taiwan

Serial Number: QHY157001   2001, November 15

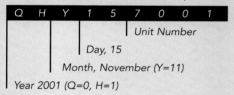

| Q | H | Y | 1 | 5 | 7 | 0 | 0 | 1 |

- Unit Number
- Day, 15
- Month, November (Y=11)
- Year 2001 (Q=0, H=1)

Note: Y2K issue came into play here. "Q" indicates the number zero for 2000.

System # A11

1997–1999
Yamaha Music Craft
Made in Japan

Serial Number: NM501J   1997, June
Every month the number started with 500.

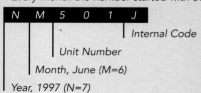

| N | M | 5 | 0 | 1 | J |

- Internal Code
- Unit Number
- Month, June (M=6)
- Year, 1997 (N=7)

Note: Same system as Custom Shop, System #A3

System # A12

1999–

Yamaha Music Craft

Made in Japan

Serial Number: PK201   1999, April

Starting in this year, each month the unit number started with 200.

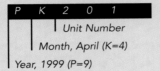

Unit Number

Month, April (K=4)

Year, 1999 (P=9)

System # A13

2001–

Yamaha Music Craft

Made in Japan

Serial Number: QIK001A   2002, April

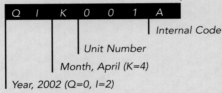

Internal Code

Unit Number

Month, April (K=4)

Year, 2002 (Q=0, I=2)

System # A14

1990–1996

YMMI (Yamaha Music Manufacturing Indonesia)

Made in Indonesia

Serial Number: 00915001   1990, September 15

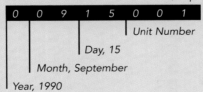

Unit Number

Day, 15

Month, September

Year, 1990

System # A15

1997–1999

YMMI (Yamaha Music Manufacturing Indonesia)

Made in Indonesia

Serial Number: 701150001   1997, January 15

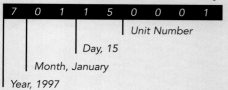

System # A16

2000–

YMMI (Yamaha Music Manufacturing Indonesia)

Made in Indonesia

Serial Number: 0001150001   2000, January 15

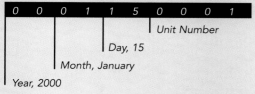

System # A17

2001–

YMMI (Yamaha Music Manufacturing Indonesia)

Made in Indonesia

Serial Number: QIH150001   2002, January 15

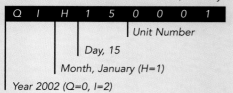

Note: The above charts include the majority of Yamaha acoustic (and acoustic-electric) and classical guitars manufactured. However, in some cases, the serial number information is no longer available and/or, for the lowest priced models, is not listed. Additionally, in some cases, exceptions to the rule will apply.

Serial Number Chart
for Electric, Archtop, and Bass Guitars

In the following charts, you can determine the year of manufacture for a Yamaha electric, archtop, or bass guitar.

The first step is to find the serial number—a combination of letters and/or numbers—and the "Made in..." label (Japan, Taiwan, Indonesia, Korea, or China) on the guitar. You should be able to find these in one of the following places: the peghead, the fingerboard at the high fret position, inside the body in the case of hollowbodies, or occasionally, in another spot on the instrument that you will need to locate.

Once you have those two pieces of information, find the country of origin and serial number in one of the following charts and, using the Letter-to-Number Reference Chart below, calculate the year of manufacture for your guitar.

LETTER-TO-NUMBER Reference Chart

Often, some of the letters in the serial numbers represent specific numbers that, in turn, stand for the month and year of manufacture. See the chart below for the code.

H	I	J	K	L	M	N	O	P	Q	X	Y	Z
1	2	3	4	5	6	7	8	9	0	10	11	12

SAMPLE

Serial Number: IM705J   1991, July

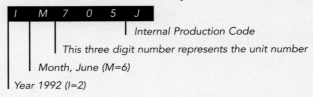

I	M	7	0	5	J

Internal Production Code
This three digit number represents the unit number
Month, June (M=6)
Year 1992 (I=2)

System # E1 (See chart on pages 132-133)
1966–1984
Made in Japan

System # E2
1984–1986
Made in Japan

Serial Number: LHQH001   1985, January

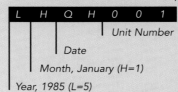

L	H	Q	H	0	0	1

Unit Number
Date
Month, January (H=1)
Year, 1985 (L=5)

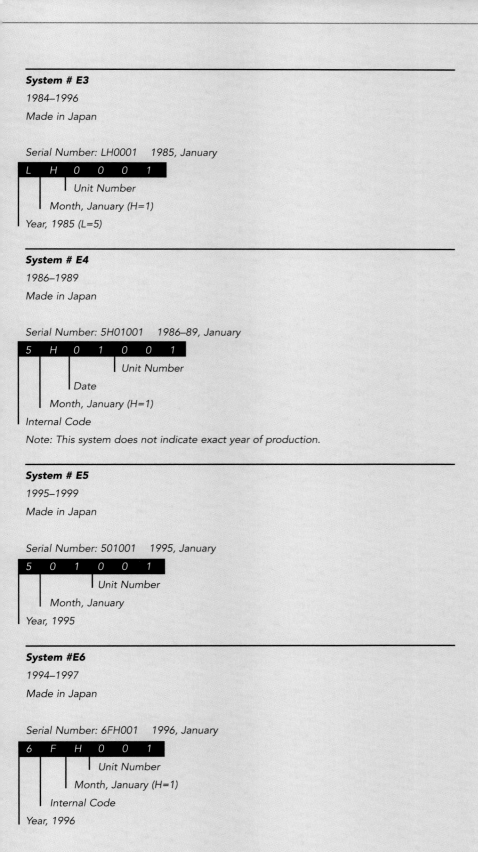

System # E3

1984–1996

Made in Japan

Serial Number: LH0001   1985, January

L H 0 0 0 1

          Unit Number

      Month, January (H=1)

Year, 1985 (L=5)

System # E4

1986–1989

Made in Japan

Serial Number: 5H01001   1986–89, January

5 H 0 1 0 0 1

            Unit Number

       Date

    Month, January (H=1)

Internal Code

Note: This system does not indicate exact year of production.

System # E5

1995–1999

Made in Japan

Serial Number: 501001   1995, January

5 0 1 0 0 1

       Unit Number

    Month, January

Year, 1995

System #E6

1994–1997

Made in Japan

Serial Number: 6FH001   1996, January

6 F H 0 0 1

         Unit Number

      Month, January (H=1)

   Internal Code

Year, 1996

System # E7

1997–

Made in Japan

Serial Number: 8FI0001   1998, February

```
8  F  I  0  0  0  1
```
        | Unit Number
     | Month, February (I=2)
  | Internal Code
Year, 1998

System # E8

1988

Made in Japan

Serial Number: SJQH001   1988, March

```
S  J  Q  H  0  0  1
```
           | Unit Number
        | Date
     | Month, March (J=3)
Internal Code

System # E9

1989–2002

Made in Japan

Serial Number: IKJK001   1994, April

```
I  K  J  K  0  0  1
S
```
           | Unit Number
        | Year, 1994 (K=4)
     | Internal Code (Japan)
  | Month, April (K=4)
Internal Code (Both I and S were used in this system.)

System # E10

2002–

Made in Japan

Serial Number: QKL001E   2004, May

```
Q  K  L  0  0  1  E
```
                 | Internal Code (E, F, I, S were used in this system.)
        | Unit Number
     | Month, May (L=5)
Year, 2004 (Q=0, K=4)

System # E11

1984–2002

Made in Taiwan

Serial Number: PM01001   1999, June 1

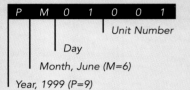

```
Unit Number
Day
Month, June (M=6)
Year, 1999 (P=9)
```

System # E12

2002–

Made in Taiwan

Serial Number: QJN010001   2003, July 1

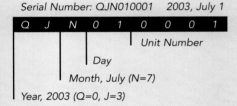

```
Unit Number
Day
Month, July (N=7)
Year, 2003 (Q=0, J=3)
```

System # E13

2003–

Made in Korea and Made in China

Serial Number: QLK0001R   2005, April

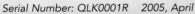
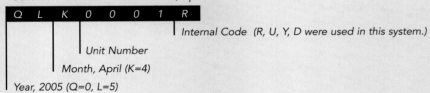

```
Internal Code  (R, U, Y, D were used in this system.)
Unit Number
Month, April (K=4)
Year, 2005 (Q=0, L=5)
```

Note: The previous charts include the majority of Yamaha electric, archtop, and bass gui-
tars. However, in some cases, the serial number information is no longer available and/or,
for the lowest priced models, is not listed.

System # E1

1966–1984

Made in Japan

The following numbering system was used for SG, SX, and BB series.

Representative Models	Serial Number Sequence	Year
SG-2, 3, 5, 7, 12	0398–3951	1966
SG-2, 3, 5, 7, 12	3952–7433	1967
SG-2A, 5A, 7A, 12A		
SG-2A, 5A, 7A, 12A	7434–10844	1968
SG-2C, 3C		
SG-2A, 5A, 7A, 12A	10645–12331	1969
SG-2C, 3C		
SG-2A, 5A, 7A, 12A	12332–13492	1970
SG-2C, 3C		
SG-2A, 5A, 2C, 3C	13493–15121	1971
SG-2A, 5A, 2C, 3C		
SG-40, 60, 80	15122–18058	1972
SG-45, 65, 85		
SG-40, 60, 80	18059–23745	1973
SG-45, 65, 85		
SG-30, 35, 45, 65		
SG-70, 90, 175	23746–36150	1974
SX-80, 125		
SG-45, 50, 70, 90		
SG-175	36151–38104	1975
SX-80, 125		
SG-175	38105–39943	1976
SX-125		

Representative Models	Serial Number Sequence	Year
SG1000	1001–1390	1976
SG2000	1001–1126	
SG1000	001391–002365	
SG2000	001251–002610	1977
BB1200	001001–001270	
BB2000	001271–001320	
SG1000	002366–003110	
SG2000	002611–003760	1978
BB1200	001321–002965	
BB2000	002001–002380	
SG1000	003111–004445	
SG2000	003761–005088	1979
BB1200	002966–004000	
BB2000	002381–002920	
SG1000	004446–005329	Through 1980 July
SG2000	005081–005375	
All Models	013001–024215	Through 1980 December
All Models	025410–059618	1981
All Models	059620–096639	1982
All Models	096640–126845	1983
All Models	126846–146196	Through 1984 July